Tools for the
Primary Care of People with
Developmental Disabilities

2011

➢ *Peer-reviewed*

➢ *Evidence-based*

➢ *User-friendly*

This publication was made possible through support from the Ontario Ministry of Community and Social Services, the Ontario Ministry of Health and Long-Term Care, and Surrey Place Centre Foundation.

To purchase copies, visit the website, e-mail, call or fax:

MUMS GUIDELINES
Tel: 416-597-6867 or toll free: 1-877-876-4580   Fax: 416-597-8574 or toll free: 1-866-540-1847
E-mail: **guidelines@mumshealth.com**   Website: **www.mumshealth.com**

Acknowledgement
The Developmental Disabilities Primary Care Initiative and Surrey Place Centre acknowledge the contribution of Medication Use Management Services (MUMS) in the development of *The Tools for the Primary Care of People with Developmental Disabilities*. We acknowledge that the overall design layout (e.g., colour, table formats, cover and other signature expressions) was developed by MUMS and is being used with their permission for this publication. This publication is a part of the MUMS 'orange book' series.

For updates and to access the tools provided in this booklet please use the link below:
www.surreyplace.on.ca/Clinical-Programs/Medical-Services/Pages/PrimaryCare.aspx.

Comment sheets are provided at the end of the document and at **www.mumshealth.com**.

Library and Archives Canada Cataloguing in Publication

Tools for the primary care of people with developmental disabilities / Developmental Disabilities Primary Care Initiative.

Includes bibliographical references.
ISBN 978-1-894332-11-8

1. Developmental disabilities. 2. Developmentally disabled – Care. 3. Mental retardation. 4. Primary care (Medicine). I. MUMS Guideline Clearinghouse II. Developmental Disabilities Primary Care Initiative

RC570.2.T66 2011   616.85'88   C2011-901743-1

While great effort has been taken to assure the accuracy of the information, Surrey Place Centre, the Developmental Disabilities Primary Care Initiative, the reviewers, publisher, printer and others contributing to the preparation of this document cannot accept liability for errors, omissions or any consequences arising from the use of the information. Since this document is not intended to replace other information, physicians are urged to consult available drug information literature before prescribing.

Citation: Developmental Disabilities Primary Care Initiative. Tools for the Primary Care of People with Developmental Disabilities. 1st ed. Toronto: MUMS Guideline Clearinghouse; 2011.

TABLE OF CONTENTS

Developmental Disabilities Primary Care Initiative (DDPCI)

This initiative has brought together family physicians and other health care professionals who practice in a variety of clinical settings, with expertise in the care of adults with developmental disabilities (DD). Their names, areas of expertise, and place of practice are listed below.

Dr. William F. Sullivan (Chair)
Family Medicine and Ethics
Toronto, ON

Dr. Joseph M. Berg
Medical Genetics and Psychiatry
Toronto, ON

Dr. Elspeth Bradley
Psychiatry
Toronto, ON

Dr. Tom Cheetham
Family Medicine
Toronto, ON

Dr. Cynthia Forster-Gibson
Family Medicine and Genetics
Mississauga, ON

John Heng
Ethics
London, ON

Dr. Brian Hennen
Family Medicine
Halifax, NS

Dr. David Joyce
Family Medicine
Vancouver, BC

Maureen Kelly
Nursing
Toronto, ON

Marika Korossy
Library Science
Toronto, ON

Dr. Yona Lunsky
Psychology
Toronto, ON

Scientific and Editorial Staff

William F. Sullivan, MD, PhD
Laurie Dunn, MSc, BScPhm
John Heng, MA
David Joyce, MD

Maureen Kelly, BScN, MPA
Marika Korossy, BA
John Pilla, MSc, BScPhm

Copy Editor

Jo-Anne Jackson, BA

Expert Review Committee of Core Developmental Disabilities Primary Care Tools

Laura Arthurs
Quest Society
Rehabilitation
Halifax, NS

Jane Bernal
Developmental Neuropsychiatry
Cornwall Partnership Trust
Truro, Cornwall, UK

J. Carolyn Graff
College of Nursing
University of Memphis
Memphis, TN, USA

Dr. Nick Kates
Psychiatry
McMaster University
Hamilton, ON

Dr. Nicholas Lennox
Director, Queensland Centre for
Intellectual and Developmental
Disabilities
University of Queensland
Brisbane, Australia

Dr. Andrew Levitas
Psychiatry
School of Osteopathic Medicine
Stratford, NJ, USA

Dr. James Meuser
Family Medicine
University of Toronto
Toronto, ON

Ruth Northway
Learning Disability Nursing
University of Glamorgan
Glyntaff, Wales, UK

Hélène Ouellette-Kuntz
Community Health &
Epidemiology
Queen's University
Kingston, ON

Dr. Walter Rosser
Family Medicine
Queen's University
Kingston, ON

Working Groups and Contributors for Primary Care Tools

Team Lead	Team Members	

General Issues in Primary Care

William F. Sullivan Family Medicine Toronto, ON	Tom Cheetham Cynthia Forster-Gibson Maureen Kelly	Elizabeth Grier Stephannie MacDonell Valerie Temple

Informed Consent

Greg Gillis Family Medicine London, ON	Maria Gitta John Heng Marika Korossy	Renata Leong William F. Sullivan Hugo Scher

Cumulative Patient Profile (CPP) and Medication Record

Tom Cheetham Family Medicine Toronto, ON	Deborah Champ Bruce McCreary William F. Sullivan Elizabeth Grier	Brian Hennen David Joyce Stephannie MacDonell

Periodic Care Checklist (PCC)

Brian Hennen Family Medicine Halifax, NS	Terry O'Driscoll Joseph M. Berg Wendell Block	Cynthia Forster-Gibson David Joyce William F. Sullivan

Health Watch Tables / Syndrome-Specific Charts

William F. Sullivan Family Medicine Toronto, ON	Joseph M. Berg Donna Cameron Cynthia Forster-Gibson	Maureen Kelly Alin Khodaverdian Marika Korossy

Behavioural and Mental Health Tools

Elspeth Bradley Psychiatry Toronto, ON	Tom Cheetham Caroll Drummond Nancy Huntley Maureen Kelly Marika Korossy	Yona Lunsky Stephannie MacDonell Shirley McMillan William F. Sullivan Margaretha Vanderwelden

Tools for Use by Caregivers to Assist with Coordination of Care

Leeping Tao Nurse Practitioner Toronto, ON	Richard Denton Emer Dudley Maureen Kelly Teresa Broda	Judith Ludlow Sandra Stemp Karen Cowan Nicole Martindale-Coke

In addition to those listed above, thank you to the participants in the DD Training Courses and DD Colloquia, and all members of the DD PCI Planning Committee and Faculty, whose valuable suggestions have been essential in the development and improvement of these tools.

Introduction

Developmental disabilities (DD) or *intellectual disabilities* are terms used synonymously in Canada (*learning disabilities* is used in the UK and the older term *mental retardation* in the USA). These terms refer to a range of conditions in which lifelong limitations in intellectual functioning and in conceptual, social, and practical skills (i.e., adaptive functioning) are noticeable before age 18 years. Estimates of the prevalence of people with DD vary between 1-3% of Canadians, and if one includes those with borderline DD, the prevalence is significantly greater. Most adults with DD reside in and receive health care in the community. The tools in this book were developed to assist primary care providers (general practitioners, family physicians, nurses, nurse practitioners) in caring for adults with DD by helping them to implement various recommendations in *Primary care of adults with developmental disabilities: Canadian consensus guidelines* (DD Guidelines).

Development Process

Participants in a DD Training Course, based on the DD Guidelines (150 participants over four years) identified challenges in implementing the recommendations of the Guidelines and recommended development of specific tools for this purpose. Several clinician-led Tools Working Groups were tasked with developing brief, practical, and evidence-informed tools to respond to these requests. Initially, six Tools Working Groups developed a set of tools that Training Course participants and faculty deemed to be priority issues. Draft versions of each tool were reviewed by two or more nationally and/or internationally acknowledged experts in relevant areas of DD medicine and, based on feedback received, the tools were finalized. Subsequently, additional tools have been developed to address practical matters related to implementing other recommendations in the DD Guidelines.

Use of Developmental Disabilities Tools and Ongoing Development

The tools in this book are meant to complement DD Guideline recommendations. Those recommendations are framed by guiding principles that inform the DD Guidelines and related tools (i.e., dignity, inter-personal relationships, and justice considerations relevant to persons with DD). The tools are organized to correspond to the DD Guidelines sections: General Issues, Physical Health Issues, and Behavioural and Mental Health Issues. Within each section, tools are listed in the order in which they arise in the DD Guidelines. Not every guideline recommendation has a corresponding tool. Tools in this book have been developed for, and in most cases by, primary care providers with helpful input from related disciplines.

Other tools not included in this book were developed primarily for and by others who work with primary care providers. For example, the Caregiver Health Assessment was developed for and by caregivers who typically work in group homes. Such tools are meant to facilitate collaboration with primary care providers. These latter tools, along with the most recent versions of tools in this book, full references and new tools, are available at **www.surreyplace.on.ca/Clinical-Programs/Medical-Services/Pages/PrimaryCare.aspx**.

We are aware of the need to update and revise these tools. We encourage readers to assist us by providing comments and suggestions regarding tools in this book and by recommending other tools they would like to see developed. This can be done by returning the completed comment page at the back of this book. We look forward to receiving your feedback and continuing support and participation.

Acknowledgements

We would like to acknowledge the sponsors of the DD Primary Care Initiative: Ontario Ministry of Community and Social Services, Ontario Ministry of Health and Long-Term Care, Surrey Place Centre, and Surrey Place Centre Charitable Foundation. Their shared financial support of this initiative since 2005 has made the development and printing of these tools possible.

A special thank you to those listed in the prior pages who have contributed so much to the development and review of these tools. Thank you also to parents of adults with DD, caregivers and in particular to persons with DD who have contributed generously in various ways to this project.

On behalf of all those who have contributed to this project, we hope that these tools will help, in some way, to improve the health and well-being of adults with DD, so that they may more fully take part in all aspects of life.

Sincerely,
William F. Sullivan, Maureen Kelly, Marika Korossy, and John Heng, Co-editors

[1]Sullivan WF, Berg JM, Bradley E, Cheetham T, Denton R, Heng J, Hennen B, Joyce D, Kelly M, Korossy M, Lunsky Y, McMillan S. Primary care of adults with developmental disabilities: Canadian consensus guidelines. Can Fam Physician 2011;57:541-53.

SECTION I:
Tools for General Issues
in Primary Care

Genetic Assessment: Frequently Asked Questions

Etiologic assessment is often helpful in planning preventive care, treatment, and management strategies. Many adults whose developmental disabilities (DD) are of unknown origin may benefit from etiologic assessment or reassessment.

Contact a local Genetics Centre for help in deciding whether to refer, and for the referral criteria and protocol.

How do I find the nearest Genetic Centre for my patient?	Contact information for Genetic Centres in Canada is available at **https://cagc-accg.ca/**.
Are there ways of determining the likelihood of a patient's having a genetic etiology for his/her DD, so as to prioritize whom I should consider referring?	The chances of individuals having a genetic etiology for their DD generally range from <u>greater</u> to <u>lesser</u> likelihood in the following order: • Family history of DD. • Congenital malformations. • Dual diagnosis (DD and co-occurring mental illness). If possible, patients should be seen by a knowledgeable psychiatrist and/or clinical geneticist who can identify those more likely to have a genetic etiology, including those with a specific pattern of behaviours or with a specific psychiatric diagnosis. • Severe to profound DD, congenital malformation(s). • Mild to moderate DD, congenital malformation(s).
Why might a genetic assessment be helpful?	**Optimal medical management** • A tailored medical and psychosocial management approach to address physical and mental health issues can be developed once the etiology is established. For example, people with Down syndrome have an increased probability of developing thyroid disease throughout their lifespan and will benefit from earlier and more regular screening than guidelines for the general population recommend. • Identifying a genetic etiology can have health management consequences for other family members. For example, in the fragile X syndrome, pre-mutation carrier males and females have the potential to develop fragile X-associated tremour/ataxia syndrome and females have an increased risk of premature ovarian failure. **Family reasons** • The patient and other family members may want information about the cause of the DD and the risk of recurrence within the family. •There can be substantial guilt about having a child with a DD. Knowing the cause can relieve parental guilt and provide reassurance. As well, with this knowledge, family members will be aware of and be able to address issues related to specific syndromes, such as by connecting with syndrome-specific organizations.

Is there a special referral form? What information is needed on the referral?	Contact or check the website of your nearest genetic centre.
	
	• Helpful information to include in a referral:
	  – Detailed reason(s) for referral.
	  – Any previous genetic test results and the date of the test(s).
	  – Copies of other pertinent investigations (e.g., MRI, echocardiogram).
	  – Name and contact information of the Substitute Decision Maker, if needed, to provide consent for genetic testing.

Are there some tests I should do, as a family physician, prior to sending a patient with DD to a genetic centre?	• Currently some genetic centres request that fragile X molecular testing and karyotype (chromosome analysis) be done before the patient is seen for genetic assessment. Microarray analysis is a much more sensitive test that is replacing the karyotype. Call the genetics centre closest to you, or visit its website, for further information as to which tests are appropriate to do prior to referral, and for access to requisitions. • The reasons for these tests and for a genetics referral should be discussed with the individual, his/her family, and/or the Substitute Decision Maker in order to obtain appropriate consent for undertaking them. • Salient clinical information should be included on the requisition form. • If you order a test and the results are abnormal (including any type of variant found on microarray or chromosome analysis and pre-mutation carrier status for fragile X), consult a clinical geneticist regarding implications and for patient and family feedback and counseling. Referral to a genetics centre is highly recommended. In some cases, parental studies may be undertaken through the genetics centre to assist in interpretation of results.
Is genetic testing covered by health insurance?	• In Canada, genetic assessment and some medical tests are covered by the provincial health care plan. The clinical geneticist may request some tests that are performed only outside Canada and may seek prior approval for payment for them from the provincial authorities. • Private labs may charge a fee to take and transport a blood sample for some tests (e.g., molecular testing). Check with the service providers in your area.
Which diagnoses can be detected through genetic testing?	• Over 900 diagnoses are currently possible through genetic testing, a number that increases annually. • Genetic testing diagnoses include single gene mutations, whole or partial chromosome duplications and deletions (including micro-duplications and micro-deletions), imprinting defects, and mitochondrial disorders. • Relevant to the population with DD, examples of diagnoses from genetic testing include Down syndrome, fragile X syndrome, Prader-Willi syndrome, Williams syndrome, Smith-Magenis syndrome and 22q11.2 deletion syndrome. Some syndrome-specific reviews are available at **www.ncbi.nlm.nih.gov/sites/genetests**.

Which diagnoses are not primarily genetically determined?	• DD can be caused by factors other than genetic conditions, including infections, exposure to toxins/teratogens, and perinatal hypoxemia or trauma. Cerebral palsy and fetal alcohol spectrum disorders are examples. • Such a diagnosis does not preclude the person from also having a genetic syndrome.
What happens when the patient and family members go for genetic testing and counseling?	• The patient and family members will meet with a genetic counselor and/or geneticist who will obtain a detailed patient and family medical history, as well as explain the reason for the genetic assessment. • A physical exam is usually done by the geneticist. This may include measurement of salient physical features (e.g., facial ones), and photography of such features (with appropriate consent) for the individual's medical record. • Possible genetic diagnoses may be reviewed and appropriate tests to help determine a diagnosis will be discussed. Consent to retrieve records may be requested. • Information will be given so that the patient and family can provide informed consent with respect to the proposed genetic testing. • Lab tests will usually be done, including blood or urine tests. In some circumstances it may be helpful to obtain other investigations such as a skin punch biopsy, X-rays, ultrasound, CT or MRI scans. Referral to other specialists may also be recommended.
How are test results communicated?	• Results are normally reported to the referring physician and communicated to the patient, family and/or Substitute Decision Maker by the geneticist. This may include providing a genetic diagnosis and offering further counseling. • Genetic changes causing DD can occur sporadically or may be hereditary. Potential consequences of a hereditary disorder, the likelihood of developing it or transmitting it to one's children, and whether there are means to prevent it or lessen any of these effects would be discussed. • Reproductive options should also be discussed at the request of the patient and/or family members.
How does management of the patient proceed?	• Management may be through the geneticist, family physician or other specialist, depending on the condition, the needs of the patient, and available resources. • If no etiology is determined, periodic reassessment is recommended.

Resources

www.geneticresourcesontario.ca This online guide for health care providers and the public includes a list of genetic centres and specific genetic services in Ontario.

www.mountsinai.on.ca/care/family-medicine-genetics-program/family-medicine-genetics-program This Canadian website gives primary health care providers current practical information regarding screening and prevention of hereditary disorders.

www.ncbi.nlm.nih.gov/sites/genetests Provides "Gene Reviews," expert-authored peer-reviewed disease descriptions.

www.askthegen.org This website of the Department of Human Genetics at Emory University, "Ask the Geneticist," answers questions about genetic concepts, and the etiology, treatment, research, testing and predisposition to genetic disorders.

"Genetics through a Primary Care Lens" at www.genetests.org/servlet/access?id=8888892&key=VVeQo6NaqTUT8&fcn=y&fw= W5jm&filename=/tools/index.html US National Institutes of Health Genetic Tools website provides background information, teaching cases, and links to other resources for primary care providers, including a section on Developmental Delay and Genetics at a Glance.

Developed by: *Cynthia Forster-Gibson, GP Practising in Clinical Genetics*

Adaptive Functioning & Communication associated with Different Levels of Developmental Disabilities (DD)

INTELLECTUAL FUNCTIONING [a, b]	ADAPTIVE FUNCTIONING [a, c] (McCreary 2005)	COMMUNICATION (Anderson 2002)
MILD IQ: 55-70 (± 5) Percentile scores: First to third Age equivalence (AE): 9-12 years Grade: up to Gr. 6	• Unskilled job capability • May need income support if jobs are scarce • Often develops stable relationships but parenting skills are poor • Decision making: likely capable of making familiar medical decisions	• Uses a variety of sentence types (simple to complex) to communicate opinions, ideas, news, events, aspirations • Vocabulary is extensive compared to adults with DD in the moderate to profound range • Uses language to initiate and interact • Conversational difficulties may exist • Uses the phone and communicates in writing • Able to understand and use abstract language but may have difficulty expressing ideas in sequence • Can usually follow meaningful, simple, 3-step commands
MODERATE IQ: 40-50 (± 5) Percentile scores: Below the first AE: 6-9 years Grade: up to Gr. 2	• Supported employment • Income support • Regular residential supervision • Help with banking and shopping • Childrearing is beyond level of understanding and capacity • Decision making: support with medical decisions is required	• Uses phrases and simple sentences to communicate for various purposes, including expression of preference, emotion, interests and experiences • Vocabulary adequate for daily functioning • Asks and responds to questions about concrete information • Some abstract language use in talking about past events • Follows meaningful 2-step commands without support
SEVERE IQ: 25-35 (± 5) Percentile scores: Below the first AE: 3-6 years Grade: up to Gr. 1	• Continuing support and supervision in residential and day care programs needed • Unable to manage family responsibilities • Decision making: not capable of making most medical decisions except if familiar with the issue and provided sufficient support	• Uses single- and two-word combinations, gestures and/or signs to indicate basic needs and to comment about his/her environment • Vocabulary limited • Gives and shows objects, points • Comprehension still limited to the immediate environment but able to understand some action words • Can follow meaningful 1-step commands with or without support (e.g., repetition, gestures)
PROFOUND IQ: < 20-25 Percentile scores: Below the first AE: 0-3 years	• Continuing 24-hour support and supervision needed • Unable to manage family responsibilities • Decision making: can be presumed to be not capable of making medical decisions	• Uses nonverbal or single words, gestures and/or signs to indicate basic needs • A few words possible • May appear non-interactive • Comprehension limited to people, objects, and events in the immediate environment • May follow some routine commands due to understanding the situation rather than the actual words

Notes

a. Understanding the intellectual abilities and adaptive functioning of persons with DD sets the stage for productive clinical encounters. This in turn leads to optimal assessments and appropriate treatments. It also promotes better partnership with persons with DD and enables them to participate in their own health care.

- Intellectual abilities include reasoning, planning, solving problems, thinking abstractly, comprehending complex ideas, and learning from experience.

- Different levels of intellectual and adaptive functioning require different types and intensity of supports and service coordination.

b. Levels of intellectual functioning are described in terms of Intelligence Quotient (IQ), Age Equivalence (AE), performance in school and percentiles.

- This information can be helpful as a general guide but does not always reflect the person with DD's individual capabilities.

c. Adaptive functioning or adaptive behaviour refers to the skills (conceptual, social, and practical) that a person with DD has to handle the common demands of everyday life. It is an indication of how independent he or she is, compared to others with DD of a similar age and level of intellectual functioning.

- Areas of adaptive functioning that are affected to varying degrees in persons with DD include self-care abilities, receptive and expressive language, social skills, understanding, learning and remembering new things, self-direction, capacity for independent living, and economic self-sufficiency.

Developed by: *Bruce Edwards, Speech-Language Pathologist, Surrey Place Centre, Valerie Temple, Psychologist, Surrey Place Centre and Laurie Dunn, Pharmacist, MUMS.*

References

1. McCreary BD. Developmental disabilities and dual diagnosis: A guide for Canadian psychiatrists, Developmental Consulting Program, Queen's University, 2005.

2. Anderson M. In: "Help me speak": Speech language pathology services provided to individuals with dual diagnosis – reference table: Communication interventions & adults with DD – level of severity and projected outcomes. State of the HART: Habilitative Achievements in Research and Treatment for mental health in developmental disabilities; April 18, 19, 20, 2002; Vancouver, BC: Interprofessional Continuing Education, University of British Columbia; 2002. pp.113-26.

Psychological Assessment: Frequently Asked Questions

What are the indicators that an adolescent or adult with a developmental disability (DD) should be considered for psychological testing? When and why would a psychological assessment be important?	Reasons to consider referring an individual for psychological testing include: • **The person is not well understood by his/her support system:** He/she is not learning well, having difficulties coping, and/or caregivers need information on how to better understand and support him/her. • **Change from an earlier assessment:** A reassessment is recommended if there has been a long interval since the last testing, or no testing in adulthood, as early results may be less stable and factors influencing the earlier testing may have changed. • **Future planning needs:** Includes vocational, education, and housing directions. For example: Can the person live independently? What are his/her current abilities and challenges? What are his/her support needs? • **Before a psychiatric diagnosis:** It may be important to know the person's level of functioning in order to put presenting symptoms in context. Some aspects of DD (e.g., a low functioning person talking to him/herself may be developmentally appropriate for his/her level of function, but it may be interpreted as a symptom of psychosis to those who do not understand the effects of the functional level). • **Significant, unexplained change in the individual's behaviour** (e.g., new onset withdrawal or aggression). • **A specific diagnosis may be needed for income support services** (e.g., for Ontario Disability Support Program [ODSP] and disability tax credits).
What types of psychological testing can be done?	• **Cognitive:** To identify level of intellectual ability, strengths, and vulnerabilities. • **Adaptive behaviour:** To determine and describe how a person functions in day-to-day life. • **Neuropsychological:** For issues such as dementia, stroke, head injury, and genetic disorders associated with cognitive decline (e.g., Down syndrome). • **Personality and psychiatric type:** As an adjunct to psychiatric care (e.g., testing for depression, anxiety, or hyperactivity).
Is psychological testing of people with DD a specialty area of psychology? Do I need to find a psychologist with special training or expertise in DD?	• For those who are *borderline to mildly impaired*, any qualified psychologist can provide testing. • For those who are *moderately or severely impaired*, ideally, a psychologist should be experienced and skilled in testing such individuals.

How do I go about finding a psychologist to do testing on my patient with DD?	• For patients under the age of 21 who are still in school, the best route is through the school board. • Local developmental services (through the Ministry of Community and Social Services, or Community Networks of Specialized Care) are generally the best resource. Consult professionals in this field in your area. • In Toronto, consult the Developmental Services Toronto (DSTO) website **www.dsto.ca**. • Elsewhere in Ontario, consult the College of Psychologists of Ontario website **www.cpo.on.ca**.
How long is the usual wait time, before my patient will be seen?	• Services provided through school boards vary, but the wait can be up to a few years. • Surrey Place Centre, which provides testing for the Toronto catchment area, has a wait time of anywhere between one to two months up to about one year depending on the type of assessment and priority given to the case. • Private testing can be arranged within a few weeks if the patient or their family has the financial resources to pay for it.
How much will this testing cost?	• **School Board:** No cost. It is important to consider obtaining an assessment while the individual is in school when the cost is covered. Records of past assessments can be requested from the school. • **Developmental Centre** (e.g., Surrey Place Centre in Toronto): No cost. • **Private:** The typical cost for a full developmental assessment is from $1,500 - $2,500. This can be paid for privately or through employer-extended health care benefits, if available.
Are there any other resources available that do not charge, or any government or other funds to help a patient pay for this testing?	• Rehabilitation, vocational placement or developmental services programs sometimes offer assessment services. • Many extended health care insurance plans (e.g., some provided by one's employer) cover psychological testing under a co-pay or partial payment basis. • A portion of payments for psychological assessment or treatment can be deducted in the individual's income tax return under health care expenses.
What information does the psychologist need in the referral?	• **Developmental history:** Especially early development – when he/she walked, talked, and toileted. • **Medical disorders:** Particularly those that can affect or interfere with cognition, including epilepsy, psychiatric diagnoses (e.g., depression, schizophrenia), and attention-deficit hyperactivity disorder (ADHD). • **Medications:** Particularly those that may affect or interfere with cognition. • **Relevant past assessments:** Psychological, psychiatric, previous brain scans (CT or MRI) or occupational therapy. • **History of exposure or injury:** Includes history of alcohol exposure in utero or past traumatic brain injuries.

What can my patient and his/her caregiver(s) expect during the appointment for psychological testing?	• The individual and caregiver will be interviewed. This typically takes one to two hours. • Testing will be done with the individual one-on-one. There may be one or more sessions of one-on-one testing that will last between one and four hours each, depending on the type of testing. • Testing will be followed by a feedback session for the individual and caregiver where the results of the testing, an explanation of what they mean, and any recommendations will be provided. This generally takes about an hour. • The patient can identify to whom he/she would like the report to be sent.
What information am I likely to receive back from the psychologist to help me in managing my patient?	• **Level of functioning:** Will include how the individual compares cognitively to others in his/her age group as well as his/her relative strengths and vulnerabilities. The information may be expressed in various ways, including standard scores (e.g., IQ range) and/or Age Equivalence (AE) scores. • **Education/placement:** Recommendations regarding education and skill development abilities and capacities, and strategies to use to help the individual learn. • **Emotional disorders, personality:** How the individual compares with others (e.g., those with a similar level of DD or with average intelligence) on various scales (e.g., depression or anxiety scales). • **Behavioural management:** May include recommendations or strategies for dealing with challenging behaviours. • **Other services:** May include recommendations regarding such services as counseling, occupational therapy, Adult Protective Services Worker and local programs.

Developed by: **Valerie Temple**, *Psychologist, Surrey Place Centre*

Informed Consent in Adults with Developmental Disabilities (DD)

Primary care providers initiate the consent process for a person with DD when:

(1) A new treatment or a change in treatment is proposed, unless it had been accepted through a previously agreed-to 'plan of care.' Consent should be obtained not only for treatment/management but also for assessment/investigation, especially if invasive. The health care provider who proposes a treatment/investigation has the obligation to obtain consent to administer it from the patient, if capable, or from his/her legally authorized Substitute Decision-Maker (SDM).

(2) There is a change in the patient's ability to understand the nature and effect of the treatment. This change can be positive as well as negative (e.g., the patient may develop new skills that facilitate their giving consent, or his/her function may deteriorate and thus require a SDM.)

STEPS INVOLVED IN THE CONSENT PROCESS

A. Determine Capacity (see Checklist C)

- **Capacity** refers to the mental ability to make a *particular* decision at a *particular* time; it is question- and decision-specific and should be documented relative to each decision. Assess capacity to consent for each treatment or plan of treatment. Even when a Power of Attorney (POA) for Personal Care exists, capacity for consent to the particular treatment at this time should be assessed.

- **Capacity is not static** but can change over time or require distinct abilities depending on the nature and complexity of the specific treatment decision. Specific capabilities may be lost or gained at different times during the life of a patient with DD. Situations may arise where consent to a treatment has been given or refused on a patient's behalf. However, if that patient then becomes capable of consenting to the treatment in the opinion of the health care practitioner, the patient's own decision would take precedence over that of the SDM.

- **Assessed capacity can vary according to the supports provided.** Involve the patient wherever possible by adapting the level and means of communicating to him/her; patients require functionally appropriate means of communication and support to realize their capacity for informed consent to, or refusal of, treatment. Offer information in a form you believe the patient will understand (e.g., pictures, symbols, gestures, vignettes). (See also *Communicating Effectively with People with Developmental Disabilities.*)

- **Involve others who know the patient best**, such as family members or paid care givers, to obtain information or to facilitate the patient's understanding and communication. Note that although paid care givers may provide valuable support for decision making, *they are not legally permitted to consent to or refuse treatment on behalf of a patient* in Ontario and in various other jurisdictions.

- **If the patient is incapable of giving consent**, or if there is uncertainty in this regard, follow appropriate legal procedures and ethical guidelines for assessing capacity. If incapable, delegate authority for decision making, which should be based on the patient's best interests in the circumstances. Generally, only patients with mild to moderate DD will be capable of consenting, whereas those with severe to profound DD will not have that capability but may be able to assent to a proposed treatment. Whenever possible, even when consent is obtained from a SDM, assent should be sought from the patient and be documented.

B. Obtain and Document Consent

- **Consent must be given voluntarily:** Allow sufficient time for the patient to understand, consider the information, and ask questions. If the patient requests additional information, provide a timely response.

- **Consent must be related to a proposed investigation or treatment and be informed by adequate disclosure:** The person obtaining consent should be knowledgeable and well-informed about the condition and proposed intervention.

- **Consent must not be obtained through fraud, coercion or misrepresentation:** The patient should not be under any duress or pain. It is important to be familiar with how the individual with DD usually exhibits pain (e.g., normal or unique pain responses), which may unduly affect decisions.

Name: _____ DOB: _____

C. Informed, Voluntary Consent Checklist and Sample Questions [a]

Inform the patient that you will be doing a capacity assessment with him/her. Do not assume that the patient will understand the connection between the illness and some consequent intervention.

Use the categories below to guide your assessment, and the examples below them if helpful.

- For each category of question, check **Yes**, **No** or **Unsure**.
- If the answer is No to any of these questions, the patient is not capable.

1. **Does the patient understand that you are offering an intervention for a health problem?**   ☐ Yes   ☐ No   ☐ Unsure

   e.g.,   What problems are you having right now?
   What problem is bothering you most?
   Do you know why you are in the hospital/clinic?

2. **Does the patient understand the nature of the proposed investigation or treatment and the expected benefits, burdens, and risks?**   ☐ Yes   ☐ No   ☐ Unsure

   e.g.,   What could be done to help you with your (specify health problem)?
   Do you think you are able to have this treatment?
   Do you know what might happen to you if you have this treatment?
   Do you know if this treatment can cause problems? Can it help you live longer?

3. **Does the patient understand possible alternative treatment options and their expected benefits, burdens, and risks?**   ☐ Yes   ☐ No   ☐ Unsure

   e.g.,   Do you know different ways that might make you better?

4. **Does the patient understand the likely effects of not having the proposed investigation or treatment?**   ☐ Yes   ☐ No   ☐ Unsure

   e.g.,   Do you know what could happen to you if you don't have this (*specify*) done?
   Could you get sicker or die if you don't have this (*specify treatment*)?
   Do you know what could happen if you have this (*specify treatment*)?

5. **Is the patient free from any duress (e.g., illness, family pressure) or pain or distress that might impair his/her capacity regarding the particular decision? (Note that a relatively minor illness can cause significant anxiety.)**   ☐ Yes   ☐ No   ☐ Unsure

   e.g.,   Can you help me understand why you've decided to accept/refuse this treatment?
   Do you feel that you're being punished? Do you think you're a bad person?
   Is anyone telling you that you should or should not get this treatment?

6. **Is the patient free from a mental health condition (e.g., mood disturbance or psychiatric illness) that may influence his/her capacity to give consent? (Note that having mental illness is not in itself an indicator of permanent incapacity. This factor may change once the mental health condition is treated.)**   ☐ Yes   ☐ No   ☐ Unsure

   e.g.,   Are you hopeful about the future?
   Do you think you deserve to be treated?
   Do you think anyone is trying to hurt and/or harm you?
   Do you trust your doctor and nurse?

Assessment:

DATE: _____   PRINT NAME: _____   SIGNATURE: _____

a. Questions adapted from: Etchells E. Joint Centre for Bioethics-Aid to Capacity Evaluation **www.utoronto.ca/jcb**

CAPABLE	**NOT CAPABLE**	**UNSURE**
If "YES" to ALL of the above, and the patient can remember the information long enough to make a decision (verify by asking him/her to explain the information to you), then consider that capability exists to consent to or refuse the proposed treatment.	If "NO" to ANY of the above, then repeat the questions; you may need to repeat this process several times to ensure that the patient understands. If the patient still does not understand, he/she is incapable and a legal Substitute Decision Maker (SDM) should be assigned (see below).	Consult family, if not already done Consider seeking a second opinion from: • Designated "capacity assessor" (e.g., for admission to long-term care and/or personal assistance services) www.ccboard.on.ca • Hospital ethicist/bioethics committee if available • Provincial regulatory College or Medical Association, especially if the decision is related to reproduction, genetic testing, chemical restraints, procedures, or end-of-life issues

D. Identify the Current Substitute Decision Maker (SDM)

If a patient is incapable of providing voluntary and informed consent, then consent must be obtained from the highest ranked eligible person identified in the hierarchy set out in the provincial regulations. That person is the Substitute Decision Maker (SDM).

The hierarchy in Ontario is as follows:

1. Guardian of the patient (under the Substitute Decision Act) with authority to provide consent to treatment
2. Power of Attorney (POA) for Personal Care (this individual may be a different person than POA for Property)
3. Representative appointed by the Consent and Capacity Board
4. Spouse/partner
5. Child older than 16 years of age/custodial parent or Children's Aid Society
6. Parent with right of access
7. Sibling
8. Any other relative (related by blood, marriage or adoption)

Note: In Ontario, **a paid care provider cannot function as a SDM,** although he/she can come to appointments and convey information.

E. Documentation

Document and Update Power of Attorney (POA) for Personal Care

- Even if a POA for Personal Care document exists, the physician should first assess present capacity of the patient before seeking the consent of the POA for Personal Care.
- Make sure to document and update the delegated POA for Personal Care, including specifying who (e.g., from social services) needs to initiate Power of Attorney delegation.
- If the parents have delegated SDM power to another caregiver, this should be documented.
- Document Plan of Care for Ongoing Treatment.
- Consent for treatment can apply over a period of time with a specified renewal period and may include items such as adjustment of medications. Having this consent and a documented plan of care is also useful for anticipated health problems, given the patient's current health status.

Document 'Circle of Care' [b, c]

- Consists of all health care providers and support personnel who are permitted to rely on a patient's implied consent to collect, use or disclose his/her health care information for the purposes of providing health care. In a physician's office this includes physicians, nurses, specialists or other health care providers to whom the physician refers the patient, and health professionals selected by the patient (e.g., pharmacist, physiotherapist). In a hospital it includes the attending physician and members of the health care team who have direct health care responsibilities to the patient.

Advance Care Planning

- Discuss with patient and his/her caregivers and record (e.g., patient's preference for SDM, Advance Directives or a Living Will).

Cross-Cultural Sensitivity

- Be respectful of cross-cultural differences in communication styles.
- Seek consultation and input from members of the patient's cultural community, as necessary, to enhance communication.

---

[b] www.mcmasterchildrenshospital.ca/body.cfm?id=209

[c] www.ipc.on.ca/images/Resources/circle-care.pdf

F. Consent Required for Incapable Patients in Various Medical Situations in Ontario

(HCCA[1], CPSO[2]) *Note: In Ontario, The Mental Health Care Act supersedes the Health Care Act.*

EMERGENCY SITUATIONS ↓	• Patient is experiencing severe suffering or is at risk of sustaining serious bodily harm if the treatment is not administered promptly. • To save life or prevent serious damage to health.
ACTION IF CONSENT NOT AVAILABLE	• Treatment [d] may be given **without consent** to an incapable patient if, in the opinion of a physician, there is an emergency and the delay required to obtain consent or refusal on the patient's behalf will prolong that patient's suffering or will put him/her at risk of sustaining serious bodily harm or death. • Inquire if the patient has Advance Directives.
NON-EMERGENCY MAJOR ↓	• Administering medications, or certain procedures (e.g., long-acting injectable hormonal substances for contraception, IUD insertion, draining an abscess). • Testing for HIV. • Providing treatment(s) for situations that pose substantial risk to the patient. • Providing procedural sedation and analgesia in the Emergency Department.
ACTION IF CONSENT NOT AVAILABLE	• If there is no SDM or he/she cannot be contacted, only the Consent and Capacity Board can give consent.
NON-EMERGENCY MINOR ↓	• Providing routine medical or dental treatments (e.g., check-up, ear syringe, nail cutting). • Administering routine medications or adjusting doses. • Providing topical anaesthetics or mild analgesia for minor procedures (e.g., laceration repair).
ACTION IF CONSENT NOT AVAILABLE	• If there is no SDM or he/she cannot be contacted then treat if patient assents or does not object, and treatment is necessary. • Make a note in the patient record that he/she is assenting or not objecting and that treatment is necessary. Obtain consent from SDM as soon as possible. • Defer or re-book.

[d] **Treatment includes:** anything performed for a therapeutic, cosmetic or other health-related purpose, treatment plan, adjustments in the treatment, and continuation of the same treatment in a different setting.

Treatment does not include: assessing the patient's capacity to make decisions about treatment, admission to a care facility or personal assistance services, assessing the patient's capacity to manage property, taking a health history, assessing or examining a patient to determine the general nature of the patient's condition, communicating an assessment or a diagnosis, admitting a patient to a hospital or other facility, providing a personal assistance service, providing a treatment that in the circumstances poses little or no risk of harm or performing anything prescribed by the regulations.

References

1. *Health Care Consent Act of Ontario*, 1996. Chapter 2, Schedule A Ontario Regulation 856/93, as amended 2007 (made under the *Medicine Act*, 1991).

2. College of Physicians and Surgeons on Ontario Consent to Medical Treatment. Policy available at **www.cpso.on.ca/uploadedFiles/policies/policies/policyitems/Consent.pdf**.

Resources

Consent: A Guide for Canadian Physicians, Third Edition, The Canadian Medical Protective Association, 1996.

The Mini Task Force on Capacity Issues, The Dementia Network of Ottawa (2007). Determining capacity to consent: Guiding physicians through capacity and consent to treatment law. *Dialogue,* 3(3) July 2007: 32-38. **www.cpso.on.ca/uploadedFiles/policies/policies/policyitems/capacity_consent_july07dialogue.pdf**

U.K. Web Resource for determining capacity for persons with developmental disabilities: **www.intellectualdisability.info/how-to../consent-and-people-with-intellectual-disabilities-the-basics/**

In Ontario: Consent and Capacity Board: **www.ccboard.on.ca**

1 800 461-2036; 416 327-4142 Direct Line in Toronto

Legal Aid Ontario: **www.legalaid.on.ca**

Office of the Public Guardian and Trustee 1 800 366-0335

Ontario Partnership on Aging and Developmental Disabilities: **www.opadd.on.ca**

Psychiatric Patient Advocate Office (PPAO): **www.ppao.gov.on.ca**

Federal and Provincial Informed Consent Legislation Websites	
Federal	**Supreme Court of Canada Re Eve [1986] 2 S.C.R. 388** http://scc.lexum.org/en/1986/1986scr2-388/1986scr2-388.html
Alberta	**Personal Directives Act, R.S.A. 2000, c. P-6** http://www.qp.gov.ab.ca/Documents/acts/P06.CFM **Dependent Adults Act, R.S.A. 2000, c. D-11** www.qp.alberta.ca/570.cfm?frm_isbn=9780779752935&search_by=link
British Columbia	**Health Care (Consent) and Care Facility (Admission) Act [RSBC 1996]** www.bclaws.ca/EPLibraries/bclaws_new/document/ID/freeside/00_96181_01
Manitoba	**The Health Care Directives Act, C.C.S.M. c. H27** web2.gov.mb.ca/laws/statutes/ccsm/h027e.php
New Brunswick	**Infirm Persons Act, R.S. 1973, c. 1-8** www.gnb.ca/0062/pdf-acts/i-08.pdf
Newfoundland and Labrador	**Advance Health Care Directives, S.N.L. 1995, c. 4-41** www.assembly.nl.ca/legislation/sr/annualstatutes/1995/A04-1.c95.htm
Nova Scotia	**Personal Directives Act 2008, c.8,s.1.** http://nslegislature.ca/legc/statutes/persdir.htm
Northwest Territories and Nunavut	**Guardianship and Trusteeship Act, S.N.W.T. 1994, c. 29,** **as duplicated for Nunavut by s. 29 of the Nunavut Act.** www.justice.gov.nt.ca/PDF/ACTS/Guardianship%20and%20Trusteeship.pdf
Ontario	**Health Care Consent Act, 1996** www.e-laws.gov.on.ca/html/statutes/english/elaws_statutes_96h02_e.htm **Substitute Decisions Act, 1992, S.O. 1992, c. 30** www.e-laws.gov.on.ca/html/statutes/english/elaws_statutes_92s30_e.htm **Trillium Gift of Life Network Act, R.S.O. 1990, c. H.20** www.e-laws.gov.on.ca/html/statutes/english/elaws_statutes_90h20_e.htm
Prince Edward Island	**Consent Treatment and Health Care Directives Act, S.P.H.I. 1996, c. C-17.2** www.gov.pe.ca/law/statutes/pdf/c-17_2.pdf
Quebec	**Civil Code of Québec (C.C.Q.), S.Q. 1991, c. 64 (Articles, 12, 15, 20 and 22)** http://www.canlii.org/en/qc/laws/stat/sq-1991-c-64/latest/sq-1991-c-64.html
Saskatchewan	**The Adult Guardianship and Co-decision-making Act, S.S. 2000, c. A-5.3** www.justice.gov.sk.ca/Adult-Guardianship-and-Co-decision-making-Act
Yukon	**Decision Making, Support and Protection to Adults Ac, SY 2003, c.21** www.gov.yk.ca/legislation/acts/dmspa.pdf#page=30

Communicating Effectively with People with Developmental Disabilities (DD)

- People with developmental disabilities (DD) are likely to have communication difficulties.

- It will generally take more time to communicate.

- An assessment of language skills helps to choose the level of language to use. Talking with someone with a mild DD is very different than talking with a person with a moderate or severe DD.

- Many people with DD have stronger receptive (understanding) communication skills than expressive skills. Assume that the person with DD can understand more than he/she can communicate.

- Conversely, the person's expressive speech may sometimes give an impression of better comprehension than is actually the case, so check the person's understanding.

- People with DD have a variable, and sometimes limited, ability to interpret their internal cues (e.g., need to urinate, anxiety). They may not be able to give you an accurate picture of their feelings and symptoms. Involving caregivers who know the person well may help you to better understand his/her subjective experiences. However, continue to focus your communication efforts on the person rather than his/her caregiver.

- If you are in a busy area with many distractions, consider moving to a quieter location to minimize environmental distraction.

GOAL	SUGGESTED COMMUNICATION TIPS
ESTABLISHING RAPPORT *SPEAK DIRECTLY WITH THE PERSON* *AVOID TALKING TO AN ADULT AS IF HE/ SHE WERE A CHILD*	• Speak directly to the person with DD, not to his/her caregiver(s). • Ask the person: "Do you want your support worker to stay here for this visit?" • Explain at the outset the purpose and process of the meeting in simple terms. • Ask simple introductory questions (e.g., name, reason for visit). • Gain the person's attention and eye contact if possible by using his/her name or by touching his/her arm prior to speaking. • Determine how they communicate: "How do you say Yes? No?" "Do you use a device? Can you show me how to use this book/machine?" • If the person uses a communication technique or device, involve a caregiver who is familiar with it. • Show warmth and a positive regard. • Encourage the use of "comforters" (e.g., favourite item the person likes to carry, or a preference for standing and pacing rather than sitting). • Show interest in a precious object the person is holding on to. • Some people (e.g., with autism spectrum disorders [ASD]) prefer to avoid eye contact. This should be respected. • Use positive reinforcement and focus on the person's abilities rather than disabilities.

GOAL	SUGGESTED COMMUNICATION TIPS

CHOOSING APPROPRIATE LANGUAGE
 	
USE CONCRETE LANGUAGE
 	
AVOID SHOUTING
	• Use plain language. Avoid jargon.
	• Use short, simple sentences.
	• Use concrete as opposed to abstract language, for example:
	    "Show me"; "Tell me"; "Do this" (with gesture); "Now."
	    "Come with me"; "I'm going to…"
	• Use "Put your coat on" instead of "get ready."
	• Use "Are you upset? Are you sad? Are you happy?" instead of "What are you feeling?"
	• The concept of time is abstract and may be difficult to comprehend. Use examples from daily and familiar routines (e.g., breakfast, lunch, dinner, bedtime).
	• Ask or test whether the person wants you to refer to him or her in the third person (e.g., he, she, or name) rather than the second person (e.g., you).

LISTENING *LISTEN TO WHAT THE PERSON SAYS* *ALLOW ENOUGH TIME*	• Let the person know when you have understood. • Tell him or her when you do not understand. • Be sensitive to cues and tone of voice. • It may be difficult to read facial expressions or body language because of differences in muscle tone. You may need to check/validate your perceptions. • Tell the person when you do not understand him/her. • Be aware that the visit will likely take more time than usual and that several consultations may be required to complete a full assessment.

EXPLAINING CLEARLY
 	
EXPLAIN WHAT WILL HAPPEN BEFORE YOU BEGIN
 	
TELL AND SHOW WHAT YOU ARE GOING TO DO AND WHY
	• Speak slowly. Do not shout.
	• Pause frequently, so as not to overload the person with words.
	• Give the person with DD enough time to understand what you have said and to respond.
	• Rephrase and repeat questions, if necessary, or write them out.
	• Check understanding. Ask the person:
	    "Can you explain what I just said?"
	    "Can you explain what I am going to do and why?"
	• If you are unsure whether the person has understood, ask, "Can you repeat what I said in your own words?"

COMMUNICATING WITHOUT WORDS *USE VISUAL AIDS* *ACT OR DEMONSTRATE*	• People with poor language understanding rely on routines and cues from their environments to understand or anticipate what will happen. • Use pictures or simple diagrams and gestures (e.g., basic sign language). • Some people with DD may express themselves only in writing. • Allow them to handle and explore equipment. • Act out actions or procedures. • Use picture language when explaining; find signs in their communication book: "It looks like …" (point to objects familiar to the person with DD). • Point to a body part or mime a procedure (e.g., checking ears).

Resources

The Easy Health Organization in the U.K. has developed downloadable leaflets to help physicians talk with patients in plain language about common conditions: **www.easyhealth.org.uk**.

The hospital communication book (2008). Developed with the Surrey Learning Disability Partnership Board (U.K.), this is a practical guide to help people who have difficulty communicating due to impairments with learning, sight, hearing, or speech, to get equitable service in hospital. It contains clear pictures that can aid communication with health professionals: **www.mencap.org.uk/document.asp?id=1480**.

References

1. Bradley E, Lofchy J. Learning disability in the accident and emergency department. Advances in Psychiatric Treatment 2005, 11:45-57.

2. Chew KL, Iacono T, Tracy J. Overcoming communication barriers – working with patients with intellectual disabilities. Aust Fam Physician 2009 Jan-Feb;38(1-2):10-14. **www.racgp.org.au/afp/200901/200901chew.pdf**.

3 Lennox N, Beange H, Davis R, Survasula L, Edwards N, Graves P et al. Developmental Disability Steering Group. Management guidelines: Developmental disability. 2005. Version 2 Therapeutic Guidelines Limited, Victoria, Australia.

4. McCreary BD. Developmental disabilities and dual diagnosis: A guide for Canadian psychiatrists, Developmental Consulting Program, Queen's University, 2005.

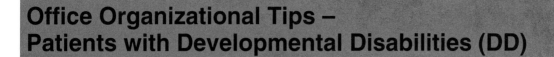

Office Organizational Tips – Patients with Developmental Disabilities (DD)

Pre-Appointment Preparations

Primary Care Provider Preparations

- While the focus of relationship building and communication should be on the patient with DD, it is also important to establish a relationship with, and obtain information from, the patient's main caregivers (e.g., family, group home staff and manager).

- Consider inviting caregivers who know the patient well to come for a pre-appointment visit. Provide them with the Caregiver's Health Assessment tool prior to the first visit so that they can complete as much as possible prior to the appointment.

- Explain to caregivers the importance of ensuring that the person who accompanies the patient with DD is reliable and familiar with the patient's current health issues.

- Try to alleviate the anxiety of the patient with DD by asking caregivers to bring to the appointment a familiar and comforting object from home (e.g., music, book).

General Office Preparations

- Meet with office staff to discuss office organization and accommodations for visits by specific patients with DD.

- Assess the physical access to the office and equipment required prior to the appointment.

- Check accommodations that may need to be made (e.g., for some patients with autism, taking off one's glasses may be important, or for patients with pica, removing objects from the waiting and examining rooms that could be eaten).

- For patients with DD who are quite anxious about visits to the doctor:
  - Have patients visit the office at least once and, if possible, two to three times, to acclimatize themselves to the office and for an introductory 'meet and greet' session. Such initial visits should only involve meeting staff and getting used to sounds and smells (i.e., no examinations or treatments).
  - Encourage caregivers to drop in with patients with DD to allow them to become familiar with the environment.

- Reduce stress by respecting the patient with DD's limits (i.e., it may take several visits to complete a physical exam).

- Take a proactive approach to avoid potential difficulties (e.g., by using rewards or distractions).

Initial Office Appointment

Allow sufficient time to assess the patient with DD's communication skills and to establish rapport (may need to book a double appointment).

- Be prepared to end an appointment early if it becomes distressing to the patient with DD.
- For patients with autism, book a time for the appointment that least disrupts their daily routines.
- Inform your office staff when a new patient with DD will be arriving. Schedule the visit time to minimize the waiting. Instruct staff to take the patient with DD and caregiver(s) directly to an appropriate room.
- Greet the patient with DD first. Ask whether you may use their first name and whether the caregiver(s) can stay.
- Inform patients with DD that you may later ask whether you can examine them alone.
- Agree on an agenda at the beginning of the visit with all present.

Follow-up Visits

- It may take a few visits to understand adequately a complicated medical history and to establish mutual trust in order to allow uncomfortable or invasive examinations.
- Corroborate the history with different caregivers involved in the life of the patient (e.g., group home and day program workers), either during office visits and/or through later telephone conference calls.
- Specific advanced preparation and coaching may be necessary for intrusive examinations (e.g., pelvic examinations in women). For further information, see the resources below.

If exams and investigations are needed

- Ask permission to proceed before any intrusion of the patient with DD's personal space.
- Explain and warn the patient about what to expect from procedures that may need to be done immediately.
- Ask caregivers whether individual care plan or protocols have been established for some procedures (e.g., venipuncture) and follow these.
- Provide reassurance during the procedure.
- For bloodwork, X-rays or physical exams, some patients may require various strategies that may include social stories about this exam, continued reassurance and support, and a desensitization plan.
  - For patients with DD who are resistant to a physical exam, consider gradual repeated exposure to the office and instruments such as the exam table and blood pressure cuff. Eventually, when patients with DD feel safe enough, invite them to lie down on the examination table.
- Use of topical anaesthetics, such as EMLA cream (apply at least one hour before procedure) or a sedative medication, such as lorazepam, may be helpful prior to distressing procedures, such as blood tests and radiological investigations.

Referrals

- When referring, identify that this is a patient with DD. Send as much information as possible, including any adaptations, accommodations or communications that you have found helpful with this patient (i.e., all the information you would like at a first visit).

- Consider a direct telephone call with the specialists concerned so that they understand the referral question and the complexities that may be faced in evaluating particular patients with DD.

- It may be helpful to network with other physicians in your area who care for patients with DD. They may know and have worked with specialists who are especially accommodating and knowledgeable regarding patients with DD.

- If a referral is made for a specialist consultation, consider deferring blood tests until after the appointment so that all tests can be undertaken at one time.

- Keep track of referrals made until consultation reports are received.

Prescriptions

- Send a copy of any new prescription to the patient with DD's pharmacist, maintain a copy on the chart, and provide the patient or caregiver with a copy.

Resources

Autism Steering Committee – North Shore LIJ. *Your next patient has autism*, and other resources regarding autism spectrum disorders for health care professionals. **www.northshorelij.com/NSLIJ/autismtoolkit**

Simpson, KM. Table Manners and Beyond – The Gynecological Exam for Women with Developmental Disabilities and Other Functional Limitations. **www.bhawd.org/sitefiles/TblMrs/cover.html**

Witemayer S. Gyn Exam and Mammograms for Women with DD's. – Recommendations for routine gynecologic examinations and mammograms for women diagnosed with DD's. **http://hsc.unm.edu/som/coc/resources/articles/GYN.pdf**

References

1. Bradley E, Lofchy J. Learning disability in the accident and emergency department. Advances in Psychiatric Treatment 2005;11:45-57.

2. Lennox N, Beange H, Davis R, Survasula L, Edwards N, Graves P et al. Developmental Disability Steering Group. Management Guidelines: Developmental Disability. 2005. Version 2 Therapeutic Guidelines Limited, Victoria, Australia pp. 7-27.

TODAY'S VISIT

**Main Reason for Today's Visit to the Physician or Nurse
(To be filled out by the Patient with DD and Caregiver)**

- Please bring an updated form for each visit to the physician/nurse.
- Bring an updated medication list, or all medications being taken.
- Bring any monitoring forms being used (i.e., sleep or behaviour charts).
- Keep a copy of this completed form for the patient's home medical files.

Up-to-date Medication List attached? ☐

Name: _____ Gender: _____
(last, first)

Address: _____

Tel. No: _____

DOB (dd/mm/yyyy): _____

Health Card Number: _____

Date of Visit: _____

Patient / Caregiver (see back of page)

What is the main health problem the patient with DD or caregivers are concerned about?

When did it start?   List any new symptoms.   List possible contributing factors.

Circle or list other needs – e.g., prescription renewals, test results, forms to be filled out, appointment for annual exam

Any Recent Changes or Stressors?   ☐ **No** ☐ **Yes:** _____
(e.g., staff changes, family illness or stress, changes in living or social environment)

Any recent visit to the dentist or other doctor?   ☐ **No** ☐ **Yes:** _____
Any recent medication changes or additions?   ☐ **No** ☐ **Yes:** _____
(include antibiotics, creams or herbal medicines)

Caregiver Needs – Write down or tell doctor or nurse whether there are issues regarding caregiver fatigue or burnout

Name/Position:	**Contact #:**	**Signature:**

**PHYSICIAN / NURSE TO COMPLETE, KEEP COPY FOR CHART,
AND GIVE COPY TO THE PATIENT / CAREGIVER**

Physician / Nurses

Assessment:

Treatment Plan including Medication Changes:

Advice to Patient and Caregivers:

Next Planned Visit / Follow-Up: _____   **MD / RN Signature:** _____

Recent Changes? **If yes, check and briefly describe.** *Complete appropriate sections of monitoring chart below*

☐ **Activity level**   ☐ **Mobility**

☐ **Sleeping habits**   ☐ **Pain or distress**

☐ **Eating patterns/Weight change**   ☐ **Swallowing**

☐ **Bowel routine**   ☐ **Mood or behaviour**

☐ **Other:** _____

MONITORING OF DAILY FUNCTIONS DURING THE PAST WEEK

	MON.	TUES.	WED.	THURS.	FRI.	SAT.	SUN.
ACTIVITY LEVEL (N, ↓ or ↑)							
SLEEP Pattern and Hours required *(daytime and night)*							
EATING/ WEIGHT (N, ↓ or ↑) Include total # of meals and # completed/day							
BOWEL ROUTINE (N, ↓, ↑, C)							
MOOD/ BEHAVIOUR (N, ↓ or ↑) Describe if changed (e.g., agitated, withdrawn)							

Fill in chart using: **N = Normal** or usual for that person;   ↓ **= Decrease** in amount, level or function;   ↑ **= Increase** in amount, level or function
C = Constipation – *a stool is passed less often than every two days or stools are hard and/or difficult or painful to pass, even if the person has stools many times per week.*

Advocacy Role of Family Physician/Advanced Practice Nurse
in Caring for Patients with Developmental Disabilities (DD)

Care for patients with DD needs to be **person-centred**.

- Patients with DD need equitable access to health care without discrimination because of their disabilities.

- Decisions about health interventions should take into account medical benefits and risks and also particular needs and circumstances, and should provide patients with DD the opportunity and support they need to participate in making informed health care decisions.

The **full range of service options** needs to be available locally for the patient to help him/her **achieve optimal quality of life**, including:

- Case management

- Housing

- Support at home

- Meaningful daytime activity, education or work

- Advocacy

- Generic and specialist health care

Training of caregivers may be needed to ensure **appropriate expectations for the individual and improve supports.**

- Understand the causes/contributors to the behaviour, triggers, and behavioural interventions to help the patient.

- Adjust caregiver expectations so they can work more effectively with the patient.

- Provide more appropriate support and make environmental changes to help the patient, e.g., increasing or reducing sensory stimulation as needed.

Where service gaps are identified for patients with DD and significant behavioural problems, the primary care provider and case manager should communicate these to the responsible program manager in:

- Currently, the regional Ministry of Community and Social Services – *after July 1, 2011*, the regional "Developmental Services Ontario" contact agency.

- The Community Networks of Specialized Care (**www.community-networks.ca**).

- Work with the system to identify and find strategies to resolve the issue.

In their role as advocate for people with DD, primary care providers need to know about laws, regulations, policies and initiatives that are in place for people with DD and their caregivers.

In Ontario, two major initiatives in 2011 focus on improving social inclusion and quality of life for people with DD: quality assurance regulations and one designated agency as the single point of contact in each of the nine regions. **www.mcss.gov.on.ca/en/mcss/programs/developmental**

1. On January 1, 2011, new regulations on 11 quality assurance measures came into force for agencies providing care to people with DD. Go it **www.e-laws.gov.on.ca/html/regs/english/elaws_regs_100299_e.htm**.
   Areas include:
   - Abuse prevention and reporting[1]
   - Notification of incidents of abuse
   - Implementation of measures promoting social inclusion
   - Individual Support Plans (ISPs)
   - Assistance with management of finances
   - Health promotion, medical services, medication, nutrition and diet, fitness and hygiene
   - Confidentiality, privacy and consent
   - Safe environment
   - Safety and security of persons with DD
   - Human resource practices

   There are an additional 18 key requirements for residential services and supports that are outlined.

2. Starting July 2011, adults with a developmental disability will access a single point of contact in their region to apply for services and supports. These new regional contact points, which will be known as "Developmental Services Ontario," will be a single window to provide information, confirm eligibility for service and supports, determine service and support needs, and link people to services and supports in their community. **www.mcss.gov.on.ca/en/mcss/programs/developmental/improving/new_application.aspx**

---

[1]**Abuse prevention and reporting:** Agencies shall promote zero tolerance of all forms of abuse. People with disabilities are to receive abuse education, to be able to make choices for themselves, and take action to protect themselves. All staff and volunteers with direct contact are to receive training on abuse prevention, identification and reporting. Under the regulation, it is mandatory that all abuse be reported to the police immediately. Situations in which the Substitute Decision Maker must be notified are outlined.

Community Resources in Ontario
for Adults with Developmental Disabilities (DD), including Mental Health Resources

Ministry of Community and Social Services (MCSS) – Developmental Services Branch:
Developmental Services fall under the umbrella of MCSS

- Ontario is divided into nine regions with a Regional Director for each regional office
- Services and supports for adults with DD, 19 years and older, include:
  - transition for young adults leaving school
  - community, financial, employment, residential and family supports
  - case management

If the adult with DD does not have a case manager and appropriate services, contact the Regional MCSS Office at 1-866-340-8881(toll-free main number) or go to **www.mcss.gov.on.ca/en/mcss/regionalmap/regional.aspx**.

Starting July 1, 2011, under the new umbrella of "Developmental Services Ontario", a single agency will serve as the regional contact and service coordination point in each of the nine provincial regions. Go to **www.mcss.gov.on.ca/en/mcss/programs/developmental/improving/new_application. aspx**.

Community Networks of Specialized Care (CNSC) www.community-networks.ca

- Coordinate specialized services for adults with DD with behavioural or mental health issues (dual diagnosis).
- Each regional Network has a CNSC Coordinator who works with local community agencies and mental health service providers to coordinate access to appropriate services.
- They can be a very helpful starting point for accessing services for patients with DD and complex behavioural/mental health issues.

ConnexOntario – Mental Health Service Information Ontario (MHSIO) www.mhsio.on.ca

- This province-wide information and referral service provides Ontarians with round-the-clock access to information about mental health services and supports.
- Funded by the Ontario Ministry of Health and Long-Term Care (MOHLTC).
- Designed to link callers with suitable options tailored to their individual needs.
- MHSIO operates a confidential and anonymous Information Line (1-866-531-2600) which is available 24 hours a day, seven days a week.

Respite Services for Families in Ontario www.respiteservices.com
Lists respite programs and services for children and adults in Ontario, by location.

CAMH (Centre For Addiction And Mental Health) http://knowledgex.camh.net
Effective July 2011, a new toolkit for primary care providers will be posted on the CAMH Knowledge Exchange website. It was developed by CAMH, Surrey Place Centre and the CNSCs, with input from primary care providers. This toolkit will list the resources needed to help primary care patients with DD and their caregivers, and will include resources for situations of behaviour concerns or crises.

SECTION II:
Physical Health Tools

CUMULATIVE PATIENT PROFILE

For adults with developmental disabilities (DD)

Adapted from template originally developed by the Department of Family and Community Medicine, Faculty of Medicine, University of Toronto, and Electronic Medical Record, DFCM, St. Michael's Hospital, Toronto

Name: _____ **Gender:** _____
(last, first)

Address: _____

Tel. No: _____

DOB (dd/mm/yyyy): _____

Health Card Number: _____

Initial Assessment Completed:
____/____/_____
dd   mm   yyyy
Consider annual review, and update sooner when changes occur, e.g., decision-making capacity

Prefers to be called: _____

Etiology of DD: _____ ☐ Definite ☐ Probable ☐ Possible ☐ Unknown

Genetic assessment: ☐ No ☐ Yes **Date:** ____/____/____
dd   mm   yyyy

Report on file? ☐ No ☐ Yes: _____

Psychological assessment: ☐ No ☐ Yes **Date:** ____/____/_____ **Report on file?** ☐ No ☐ Yes
dd   mm   yyyy

Level of adaptive functioning: ☐ Mild ☐ Moderate ☐ Severe ☐ Profound ☐ Unknown

Decision-Making Capacity

Decision-Making Capacity: *Capacity to consent may vary over time and with the type of decision. Assess when proposing interventions for which consent is required. [Guideline 7] See Informed Consent Tool*

☐ Capable ☐ Not capable ☐ Unsure

Substitute Decision Maker (SDM):

Name: _____ Contact Information: _____

Next of Kin (if not SDM):

Name: _____ Contact Information: _____

Others who may be helpful in decision making (e.g., Guardian, Power of Attorney for Personal Care, Office of the Public Guardian and Trustee, helpful agencies/support persons):

SPECIAL NEEDS AND COMMUNICATION

Usual Clinic Visit Routines: ☐ Prefers early day ☐ Prefers end of day ☐ Limit time in waiting room

☐ Special positioning for exam ☐ Extra staffing needed ☐ May require sedation

Tolerates venipuncture? ☐ Yes ☐ No

☐ Other: _____

Expressive Communication (method, devices):

Receptive Communication – prefers:
☐ Pictures ☐ Simple explanations ☐ Written ☐ Sign language ☐ Other: _____

Triggers (e.g., trauma, noise, lighting, smells, colour, textures): _____

Response Behaviours: **How to help:**

Usual Response to Medical Exam: ☐ Fully/partially cooperates ☐ Fearful ☐ Resistant ☐ Aggressive

Usual Response to Pain or Distress: ☐ Normal ☐ Unique (describe):

Cautions (e.g., aggression, pica, aspiration risk): – specify modifications, precautions

	Date	Billing Code	PROBLEM LIST – Current Problems (description, date identified, associated diagnoses)
PROBLEM LIST			

CURRENT MEDICATIONS

	Start Date	Name of Medication and Directions (dose, route, frequency, any specific instructions) Asterisk(*) to indicate if repeatable
CURRENT MEDICATIONS		

RECORD OF PAST MEDICATIONS

Start Date	Stop Date	Name of Medication and Directions (dose, route, frequency, specific instructions)	Comments Reason for discontinuation (e.g., ineffective, adverse effect, treatment complete)

ALLERGIES (include medications, food, stinging insect, pollen and dander, other)

Allergy	Medication Reaction Type (allergy, side effect, exaggerated, other effect)	Reaction Severity (life threatening, major reaction, minor reaction, no reaction)	Status (confirmed, suspected)	Brief Description of the Reaction	Treatment Details (optional)

IMMUNIZATION	Year	Year	Year	Year
Influenza Immunization				
			Pneumovax	

Family History	Patient's Past History (including hospitalizations)

IMMUNIZATIONS

FAMILY and PAST HEALTH HISTORY

PERSONAL HISTORY

PERSONAL HISTORY

Living Situation: ☐ Family ☐ Group home ☐ Foster home ☐ Independent ☐ Other: _____

Most important relationships:

Caregivers and supports:

Employment or Day Program (indicate total hours/week):

Leisure Activities:

Nutrition, Dietary:

Exercise:

Sexually active:

Past ☐ No ☐ Yes ☐ Unknown

Current ☐ No ☐ Yes ☐ Unknown

RISKS

RISKS

Tobacco

Alcohol

Street Drugs

Behaviour

REMINDERS (include exams indicated, e.g., vision, hearing, dental, psychology/genetic reassessment, cancer screening)

Periodic Tests	Date	Date	Date	Date	Date	Comments or follow-up

REMINDERS

Advance Planning Needs:

☐ Transition ☐ Crisis ☐ Palliative ☐ End of Life ☐ DNR If yes, record on file?

☐ Other: _____

Preventive Care Checklist Form
for adult females with a developmental disability (DD)

⚥

Original developed by: Dr. V. Dubey, Dr. R. Mathew, Dr. K. Iglar.
Adapted with permission by the DD Primary Care Initiative 2011

Please note:
Bold = Good evidence
(Canadian Task Force on Preventive Health Care)
Italics = Fair evidence
(Canadian Task Force on Preventive Health Care)
Plain text = Guidelines (other Canadian sources)
Highlighted = Differences with respect to DD
– refer to Explanations sheet.

Name: _____
(last, first)

Address: _____

Tel. No: _____

DOB (dd/mm/yyyy): _____

Health Card Number: _____

Date of Visit: _____

Etiology of DD, if known:

Capacity to consent:

☐ Capable   ☐ Guardian   ☐ Substitute Decision Maker

☐ Power of Attorney   ☐ Public Guardian & Trustee

Advance Care Planning Needs:

Living Situation:

☐ Family ☐ Group home ☐ Foster home ☐ Independent
☐ Other: _____

Update Cumulative Patient Profile ☐ **Medications**
☐ Family History   ☐ Communication
☐ Hospitalizations/Procedures   ☐ Allergies

Current Concerns

Lifestyle/Habits
Diet: *Smoking:*
  Fat /Cholesterol   *Alcohol:*
  Fibre   Illicit Drugs:
  Calcium
  Sodium   *Sexual History:*
Exercise/Obesity: Family Planning/ Contraception:
Day Program/Work:
Family: Sleep:
Relationships (recent changes?):

Functional Inquiry

	Normal	Remarks
HEENT:	☐	
CVS:	☐	
Resp:	☐	
GI:	☐	Screen: GERD, constipation, *H.pylori*
GU:	☐	
Sexuality Issues:	☐	
MSK/mobility:	☐	
Fall assessment *(if indicated):* ☐		
Derm:	☐	
Neuro:	☐	

	Normal	Remarks
Cognitive Changes:	☐	
functional assessment (if indicated)		
dementia screen (if indicated)		
Behavioural Changes:	☐	
difficult or challenging behaviours		
possible pain or distress		
possible abuse or neglect or exploitation (screen annually)	☐	
Mental Health:	☐ *Depression screen* ☐ +ve ☐ -ve	
Constitutional Symptoms:	☐	

EDUCATION / COUNSELING

Health Behaviours:
☐ **folic acid (0.4-0.8 mg OD, for childbearing women)**
☐ *adverse nutritional habits*
☐ *dietary advice on fat/cholesterol (30-69 yrs)*
☐ adequate calcium intake (1000-1500 mg/d) [1]
☐ adequate vitamin D (400-1000 IU/d; 800-1000 IU/d > 50 yrs)
☐ *regular, moderate physical activity*
☐ *weight loss counseling if overweight*
☐ *avoid sun exposure, use protective clothing*
☐ *safe sex practices/STI counseling*

Alcohol   ☐ Yes ☐ No
☐ *case finding for problem drinking*
☐ *counseling for problem drinking*

Smoking   ☐ Yes ☐ No
☐ **smoking cessation**
☐ **nicotine replacement therapy**
☐ *dietary advice on fruits and leafy green vegetables*
☐ *referral to validated smoking cessation program*

Personal Safety
☐ **noise control programs**
☐ **hearing protection**
☐ *seat belts*
☐ bicycle helmets
☐ propensity to ingest noxious substances (pica)

Oral Hygiene (q6mths)
☐ regular dental care
☐ ***brushing/flossing teeth***
☐ **fluoride (toothpaste/ supplement)**
☐ *tooth scaling and prophylaxis*
☐ ***smoking cessation***

Please note:

Bold = Good evidence
(Canadian Task Force on Preventive Health Care)

Italics = Fair evidence
(Canadian Task Force on Preventive Health Care)

Plain text = Guidelines
(other Canadian sources)

Highlighted = Differences with respect to DD
– refer to explanation sheet which follows.

Name:

Physical Examination

HR: *BP:*   RR: HT(cm):   WT(kg):   BMI: _____ or Waist Circumference: _____ or Waist-hip ratio: _____
Hip Circumference: _____

Eyes: *Snellen sight card: R*   **Breasts:**
                                                        L   Abdo:

Nose:

Ears: *whispered voice test: R*   Ano-Rectum:
                                                        L

Mouth/Throat/Teeth: Pelvic: ☐ *Pap*

Neck/Thyroid: MSK/Joints/Scoliosis/Mobility aids:

CVS: Extremities:

Resp: Neuro:

Derm:

Age 21 and Older

Lab/Investigations	Immunization

☐ **Mammography** (50 until 69 yrs, q1-2yrs; consider if 40-49 yrs)

☐ **Hemoccult multiphase q1-2 yrs** (age ≥50)
  OR ☐ *Sigmoidoscopy* **OR** ☐ Colonoscopy

☐ *Cervical Cytology q1-3 yrs* (sexually active until age 69)

☐ **Gonorrhea**/*Chlamydia*/**Syphilis**/**HIV**/HPV [5] screen (high risk)

☐ *Fasting Lipid Profile* (≥ 50 yrs or postmenopausal or sooner if at risk) [2]

☐ *Fasting Blood Glucose, at least q3 yrs* (≥40 yrs or sooner if at risk) [3]

☐ *Bone Mineral Density if at risk 21-64 yrs* [1]; ≥ 65 yrs q 2-3 yrs if normal and q1-2 yrs if abnormal [1]

☐ Audiology assessment if indicated by screening, & q5 yrs after age 45

☐ Thyroid (TSH/T4) q 1-5 yrs if elevated risk or behaviour change

☐ **Tetanus vaccine q10yrs**

☐ **Influenza vaccine q1yr**

☐ *Rubella vaccine*   ☐ *Rubella Immunity*

☐ *Varicella vaccine (2 doses)* ☐ *Varicella Immunity*

☐ Pneumococcal vaccine (high risk or ≥ 65 yrs) [4]

☐ Acellular pertussis vaccine [4]

☐ Hepatitis B (screen/consider immunization if high risk)

☐ Hepatitis A (screen/consider immunization if high risk)

☐ Human papilloma virus vaccine (3 doses) (age 9-26) [4]

Assessment and Plans:

Date: _____   Signature: _____

References

DD references: Sullivan WF et al. Primary care of adults with developmental disabilities: Canadian consensus guidelines. Can Fam Physician 2011;57:541-53.

Unless otherwise stated, recommendations come from the Canadian Task Force on Preventive Health Care: *The Canadian Guide to Clinical Preventive Health Care.* Ottawa: Minister of Supply and Services Canada and **www.canadiantaskforce.ca**.

1. Scientific Advisory Board, Osteoporosis Society of Canada. 2010 Clinical practice guidelines for the diagnosis and management of osteoporosis in Canada: summary. *CMAJ* 2010:DOI:10.1503/cmaj.100771

2. Working Group on Hypercholesterolemia and Other Dyslipidemias. Recommendations for the management and treatment of dyslipidemia and the prevention of cardiovascular disease: 2006 update. *Can J Cardiol* 2006;22(11) 913-927.

3. Canadian Diabetes Association Clinical Practice Guidelines Expert Committee. Canadian Diabetes Assn 2003 Clinical Practice Guidelines for the Prevention and Management of Diabetes in Canada. *Can J Diabetes* 2003;27 (Suppl 2).

4. National Advisory Committee on Immunization. *Canadian Immunization Guide,* 7th edition. Ottawa: Minister of Public Works and Government Services Canada; 2006.

5. Expert Working Group on Canadian Guidelines for STIs. *Canadian Guidelines on Sexually Transmitted Infections,* 2006 edition. Ottawa: Public Health Agency of Canada.

Preventive Care Checklist Form
for adult males with a developmental disability (DD)

Original developed by: Dr. V. Dubey, Dr. R. Mathew, Dr. K. Iglar.
Adapted with permission by the DD Primary Care Initiative 2011

Please note:

Bold	= Good evidence (Canadian Task Force on Preventive Health Care)
Italics	= Fair evidence (Canadian Task Force on Preventive Health Care)
Plain text	= Guidelines (other Canadian sources)
Highlighted	= Differences with respect to DD – refer to Explanations sheet.

Name: _____
(last, first)

Address: _____

Tel. No: _____

DOB (dd/mm/yyyy): _____

Health Card Number: _____

Date of Visit:

Etiology of DD, if known:

Capacity to consent:
☐ Capable ☐ Guardian ☐ Substitute Decision Maker
☐ Power of Attorney ☐ Public Guardian & Trustee

Advance Care Planning Needs:

Living Situation:
☐ Family ☐ Group home ☐ Foster home ☐ Independent
☐ Other: _____

Update Cumulative Patient Profile   ☐ **Medications**
☐ Family History   ☐ Communication
☐ Hospitalizations/Procedures   ☐ Allergies

Current Concerns

Lifestyle/Habits

Diet: Smoking:
  Fat /Cholesterol   Alcohol:
  Fibre   Illicit Drugs:
  Calcium
  Sodium   *Sexual History:*
Exercise/Obesity: Family Planning/ Contraception:
Day Program/Work:
Family: Sleep:
Relationships (recent changes?):

Functional Inquiry

	Normal	Remarks
HEENT:	☐	
CVS:	☐	
Resp:	☐	
GI:	☐	Screen: GERD, constipation, *H.pylori*
GU:	☐	
Sexuality Issues:	☐	
MSK/mobility:	☐	
Fall assessment *(if indicated):* ☐		
Derm:	☐	
Neuro:	☐	

	Normal	Remarks
Cognitive Changes:	☐	
functional assessment (if indicated)		
dementia screen (if indicated)		
Behavioural Changes:	☐	
difficult or challenging behaviours		
possible pain or distress		
possible abuse or neglect or exploitation (screen annually)	☐	
Mental Health:	☐ *Depression screen* ☐ +ve ☐ -ve	
Constitutional Symptoms:	☐	

EDUCATION / COUNSELING

Health behaviours:
☐ *adverse nutritional habits*
☐ *dietary advice on fat/cholesterol (30-69 yrs)*
☐ adequate calcium intake (1000-1500 mg/d) [1]
☐ adequate vitamin D (400-1000 IU/d; 800-1000 IU/d > 50 yrs)
☐ *regular, moderate physical activity*
☐ *weight loss counseling if overweight*
☐ *avoid sun exposure, use protective clothing*
☐ *safe sex practices/STI counselling*

Alcohol   ☐ **Yes** ☐ **No**
☐ *case finding for problem drinking*
☐ *counseling for problem drinking*

Smoking   ☐ **Yes** ☐ **No**
☐ **smoking cessation**
☐ **nicotine replacement therapy**
☐ *dietary advice on fruits and leafy green vegetables*
☐ *referral to validated smoking cessation program*

Personal Safety
☐ **noise control programs**
☐ **hearing protection**
☐ *seat belts*
☐ bicycle helmets
☐ propensity to ingest noxious substances (pica)

Oral Hygiene (q6mths)
☐ regular dental care
☐ ***brushing/flossing teeth***
☐ **fluoride (toothpaste/ supplement)**
☐ *tooth scaling and prophylaxis*
☐ ***smoking cessation***

Please note:

Bold = Good evidence
(Canadian Task Force on Preventive Health Care)

Italics = Fair evidence
(Canadian Task Force on Preventive Health Care)

Plain text = Guidelines
(other Canadian sources)

Highlighted = Differences with respect to DD
– refer to explanation sheet which follows.

Name:

Physical Examination

HR: BP: RR: HT(cm):   WT(kg):   BMI: _____ or Waist Circumference: _____ or Waist-hip ratio: _____
Hip Circumference: _____

Eyes: Snellen sight card: R

L   Abdo:

Nose:

Ears: whispered voice test: R

L   Ano-Rectum/Prostate:

Mouth/Throat/Teeth: Genitalia:

Neck/Thyroid: Derm:

CVS: MSK/Joints/Scoliosis/Mobility aids:

Extremities:

Resp: Neuro:

Age 21 and Older

Lab/Investigations

☐ **Hemoccult multiphase q 1-2 yrs** (age ≥50)
  OR ☐ *Sigmoidoscopy* **OR** ☐ Colonoscopy
☐ **Gonorrhea**/*Chlamydia*/**Syphilis**/**HIV**/HPV [5] screen (high risk)
☐ Fasting Lipid Profile (≥ 40 yrs or sooner if at risk) [2]
☐ *Fasting Blood Glucose, at least q 3 yrs (≥40 yrs or sooner if at risk)* [3]
☐ *Bone Mineral Density if at risk 21-64 yrs* [1]; ≥ 65 yrs q 2-3 yrs if normal and q 1-2 yrs if abnormal [1]
☐ Audiology assessment if indicated by screening, & q 5 yrs after age 45
☐ Thyroid (TSH/T4) q 1-5 yrs if elevated risk or behaviour change

Immunization

☐ **Tetanus vaccine q10yrs**
☐ **Influenza vaccine q1yr**
☐ *Varicella vaccine (2 doses)* ☐ *Varicella Immunity*
☐ Pneumococcal vaccine (high risk or ≥ 65 yrs) [4,]
☐ Acellular pertussis vaccine [4]
☐ Hepatitis B (screen/consider immunization if high risk)
☐ Hepatitis A (screen/consider immunization if high risk)

Assessment and Plans:

Date: _____   Signature: _____

References

DD references: Sullivan WF et al. Primary care of adults with developmental disabilities: Canadian consensus guidelines. Can Fam Physician 2011;57:541-53.

Unless otherwise stated, recommendations come from the Canadian Task Force on Preventive Health Care: *The Canadian Guide to Clinical Preventive Health Care.* Ottawa: Minister of Supply and Services Canada and **www.canadiantaskforce.ca**.

1. Scientific Advisory Board, Osteoporosis Society of Canada. 2010 Clinical practice guidelines for the diagnosis and management of osteoporosis in Canada: summary. *CMAJ* 2010:DOI:10.1503/cmaj.100771
2. Working Group on Hypercholesterolemia and Other Dyslipidemias. Recommendations for the management and treatment of dyslipidemia and the prevention of cardiovascular disease: 2006 update. *Can J Cardiol* 2006;22(11) 913-927.
3. Canadian Diabetes Association Clinical Practice Guidelines Expert Committee. Canadian Diabetes Assn 2003 Clinical Practice Guidelines for the Prevention and Management of Diabetes in Canada. *Can J Diabetes.* 2003;27 (Suppl 2).
4. National Advisory Committee on Immunization. *Canadian Immunization Guide,* 7th edition. Ottawa: Minister of Public Works and Government Services Canada; 2006.
5. Expert Working Group on Canadian Guidelines for STIs. *Canadian Guidelines on Sexually Transmitted Infections,* 2006 edition. Ottawa: Public Health Agency of Canada.

Explanations for the Preventive Care Checklist Form — Adaptations for Adults with Developmental Disabilities

Explanations for the Preventive Care Checklist Form developed for the general adult population are available at **www.cfp.ca/cgi/content/full/54/1/84/DC1**.

The following points summarize observations more fully explained in the **Primary care of adults with developmental disabilities: Canadian consensus guidelines (2011)**. Reference is made to specific guidelines and, where pertinent, to tools developed for the care of this population, available at **www.surreyplace.on.ca/Clinical-Programs/Medical-Services/Pages/PrimaryCare.aspx**.

Note: Health Watch Tables for some syndromes have been developed, which identify health risks and recommended screening for those syndromes.

ETIOLOGY OF DD: If unknown or a previous assessment was uncertain, consider reassessment periodically, since it often informs preventive care or treatment. [Guideline 2 and *Genetic Assessment: Frequently Asked Questions*]

CAPACITY TO CONSENT: Assess capacity to consent when proposing investigations or treatments. Adapt the level and means of communicating to the patient. Support whatever decision-making capacity is possible in adults with DD. Always consider the adult with DD's best interests. [Guideline 7]

ADVANCE CARE PLANNING: Important concerning life transitions (adolescence to adulthood, adult to aging, home to residential setting), in planning for potential health-related crises and end-of-life care, and in having a clearly identified Substitute Decision Maker for issues about which a patient is incapable of providing consent. Record and review annually. [Guideline 8]

UPDATE CUMULATIVE PATIENT PROFILE
Medications: Multiple and/or long-term use of some medications may cause problems due to interactions, side effects or atypical responses, and adults with DD may be unable to communicate these occurrences. Antipsychotic medications are often inappropriately prescribed for adults with behaviour problems in the absence of a robust diagnosis of psychotic illness. [Guideline 28 and *Auditing Psychotropic Medication Therapy*]

LIFESTYLE / HABITS
Physical Inactivity and Obesity: are prevalent and associated with cardiovascular disease, diabetes, osteoporosis, constipation and earlier mortality. [Guideline 10]

Alcohol or drug abuse: Some adults with DD may have more difficulty moderating their alcohol and drug intake and experience more barriers to specialized rehabilitation services. [Guideline 30]

FUNCTIONAL INQUIRY
- **HEENT:** Vision and hearing impairments are under-diagnosed and can result in substantial changes in behaviour and adaptive functioning. [Guideline 11]

- **CVS:** Cardiac disorders are prevalent in individuals with DD. Risk factors for coronary artery disease include physical inactivity, obesity, smoking and prolonged use of psychotropic medications. [Guideline 13]

- **RESP:** Respiratory disorders (e.g., aspiration pneumonia) are among the most common causes of death among adults with DD. Swallowing difficulties are prevalent in patients with neuromuscular dysfunction or on medications with anticholinergic side effects, and may result in aspiration or asphyxiation. [Guideline 14]

- **GI:** Gastrointestinal and feeding problems are common among adults with DD. Presenting manifestations are often different than in the general population and may include changes in behaviour or weight. There may be increased risk of *H. pylori* infection. [Guideline 15]

- **Sexuality:** (e.g., menstruation, masturbation, fertility and genetic risks, contraception, menopause) is an important issue that is often not considered in the primary care of adolescents and adults with DD. [Guideline 16]

- **MSK:** Musculoskeletal disorders (e.g., scoliosis, contractures and spasticity, which are possible sources of unrecognized pain) occur frequently in patients with DD and result in reduced mobility and activity, with associated adverse health outcomes. Osteoporosis and osteoporotic fractures are more prevalent and tend to occur earlier than in the general population. Osteoarthritis is becoming more common. [Guideline 17]

- **Fall assessment:** If indicated, should include assessment of living area, mobility aids and medications (e.g., anticonvulsants, antidepressants, antihypertensives, benzodiazepines, narcotics, neuroleptics).

- **NEURO:** Epilepsy is prevalent in individuals with DD and increases with the severity of the DD. It is often difficult to recognize, evaluate and control, and has a pervasive impact on the lives of affected adults and their caregivers. [Guideline 18]

COGNITION

Functional assessment: Adaptive functioning may decline or improve in some adults with DD. A current assessment of intellectual and adaptive functioning helps to determine necessary care and supports, and establishes a baseline for future assessments. [Guideline 3 and *Psychological Assessment: Frequently Asked Questions*]

Dementia: Important to diagnose early, especially in adults with Down syndrome who are at increased risk. Diagnosis may be missed because changes in emotion, social behaviour or motivation may be gradual and subtle. A baseline of functioning against which to measure changes is needed. Differentiating dementia from depression and delirium may be especially challenging in people with DD and may require referral to a consultant. [Guideline 31]

BEHAVIOUR

Problem behaviour, such as aggression and self-injury, is not a psychiatric disorder but may be a symptom of a health-related disorder or other circumstance (e.g., insufficient supports). [Guideline 22 and *Initial Management of Behavioural Crises in Family Medicine*]

Pain and distress, often unrecognized, may present atypically in adults with DD, particularly those who have difficulty in communicating. Non-specific changes in behaviour may be the only indicator of medical illness or injury. [Guideline 4]

Abuse and neglect of adults with DD occur frequently and are often perpetrated by people known to them. Behavioural indicators that may signal abuse or neglect include unexplained change in weight, non-compliance, aggression, withdrawal, depression, avoidance, poor self-esteem, inappropriate attachment or sexualized behaviour, sleep or eating disorders, and substance abuse. [Guideline 6]

MENTAL HEALTH

Psychiatric disorders and emotional disturbances are substantially more common among adults with DD but their manifestations may mistakenly be regarded as typical for people with DD (i.e., diagnostic overshadowing). Consequently, coexisting mental health disturbances may not be recognized or addressed appropriately. [Guideline 23]

EDUCATION / COUNSELING

Adapt to the adult with DD's needs and circumstances and include caregivers.

Oral Hygiene: Dental disease is among the most common health problems encountered among adults with DD due to their difficulties in maintaining oral hygiene routines and accessing dental care. Changes in behaviour can be the result of discomfort from dental disease. [Guideline 12]

Consider the risks for the individual and adapt counseling accordingly (e.g., adults with DD have a propensity to pica, or who use a bicycle).

PHYSICAL EXAM

Some patients with DD may require adaptation of office processes and possibly desensitization over time in order to be able to cooperate in having a physical exam. [*Office Organization Tips*]

- In performing physical exam, be alert for any indicators of pain or distress. [Guidline 4]
- Ensure vision and hearing are screened, including examination for cerumen impaction. [Guideline 11]
- For patients who use a wheelchair, modified seating or other equipment like splints or orthotic devices, consult a physical or occupational therapist regarding adaptations (e.g., wheelchair, modified seating, splints, orthotic devices) and safety. [Guideline 17]
- **Cancer Screening:** Ensure that people with DD receive cancer screening appropriate to their gender, age and risk factors (e.g., breast, cervical, testicular, prostate, and colon cancer). [Guideline 21]

LAB/INVESTIGATIONS

- Refer for hearing assessment if indicated by screening and for age-related hearing loss every five years after age 45. [Guideline 11]
- Screen for **endocrine disorders** (e.g., thyroid disease, diabetes and low testosterone). [Guideline 19]

IMMUNIZATION

In addition to ensuring that adults with DD receive recommended immunizations as for the general population, consider risk of exposure to Hepatitis A and B; screen and immunize accordingly. [Guideline 20]

Health Watch Tables
for Selected Developmental and Related Disabilities

Preamble

Preventive Care Checklists (PCCs) for adult men and women are used by Canadian family physicians and other primary care providers when they perform periodic health exams. In order to help these physicians to focus on preventive health issues especially relevant to the developmental disabilities (DD) population, the PCCs have been adapted for the care of adults with DD who do not have an established etiology.

Persons with DD deserve the same quality of preventive health care as others, and so the preventive care actions applicable to the general population[1] should also be done for adults with DD, e.g., immunizations, cancer screening.

A number of specific syndromes with an established etiology and with identified health concerns were chosen for the development of specific Health Watch Tables (HWT), based on work originally undertaken by Dr. Irene Swift at the Rideau Regional Centre, Smith Falls, Ontario. These syndrome-specific HWTs were developed to complement and augment the DD Guidelines[1] and Preventive Care Checklist for adults with DD. In addition to addressing issues relevant to adults, these HWTs also include concerns applicable in childhood.

The selection of syndromes for an HWT is based on such considerations as prevalence of these disabilities, frequency of occurrence of various adverse clinical manifestations, and effectiveness of available medical interventions.

The process of developing the HWTs involved a rigorous review of existing published guidelines and of the areas of agreement and dissension among them. Full citations for all guidelines reviewed are available online for each Health Watch Table at **www.surreyplace.on.ca/Clinical-Programs/Medical-Services/Pages/PrimaryCare.aspx**.

Where best available evidence was needed to address issues not adequately covered in the guidelines, references have been cited. Given the wide variability in prevalence cited in different published studies, such figures are provided only as a base for clinical attention. Feedback from expert clinician reviewers, whose helpful input is acknowledged at the end of each HWT, has been incorporated.

Nearly all the health recommendations made in the HWTs reflect a broad consensus in published texts by specialists in the spheres under consideration. They are intended to summarize outlooks in a manner enabling busy primary care providers to undertake responsible health measures without the time-consuming requirement of having to review in detail and compare the multiple texts concerned.

The HWT recommendations are not meant to impose a rigid formula as to what must be done and when, irrespective of the primary care provider's judgement as to what is judicious in given circumstances. They attempt to highlight particular health concerns that occur more frequently among persons with various types of developmental and related disabilities than in the population as a whole.

Key websites that the primary care provider, families and caregivers may find helpful have also been included.

---

[1] Sullivan WF, Berg JM, Bradley E, Cheetham T, Denton R, Heng J, Hennen B, Joyce D, Kelly M, Korossy M, Lunsky Y, McMillan S. Primary care of adults with developmental disabilities: Canadian consensus guidelines. Can Fam Physician 2011;57:541-53.

Health Watch Table — Down Syndrome
Forster-Gibson and Berg 2011

CONSIDERATIONS	RECOMMENDATIONS
1. HEENT (HEAD, EYES, EARS, NOSE, THROAT)	
Children and Adults: Vision: ~15% have cataracts; ~ 20%-70% have significant refractive errors 5%-15% of adults have keratoconus *Hearing*: 50%-80% have a hearing deficit	☐ Neonatally: refer immediately to an ophthalmologist if the red reflex is absent or if strabismus, nystagmus or poor vision is identified ☐ Arrange ophthalmological assessment: first by 6 months for all; then every 1-2 years, with special attention to cataracts, keratoconus, and refractive errors ☐ During childhood: screen vision annually with history and exam; refer as needed ☐ Arrange auditory brainstem response (ABR) measurement by 3 months if newborn screening has not been done or if results were suspicious ☐ During childhood: screen hearing annually with history and exam; review risks for frequently occurring serious otitis media ☐ Undertake auditory testing: first at 9 – 12 months, then every 6 months up to 3 years, annually until adulthood, then every two years
2. DENTAL	
Children and Adults: tooth anomalies are common Increased risk of periodontal disease in adults	☐ Undertake initial dental exam at 2 years, then every 6 months thereafter. Encourage proper dental hygiene. Refer to an orthodontist if needed ☐ Undertake clinical exams every six months with referral, as appropriate
3. CARDIOVASCULAR	
Children: 30%-60% have congenital heart defects (CHD)	☐ Newborn screening: Obtain an echocardiogram and refer to a cardiologist, <u>even in the absence of physical findings</u> ☐ In children and adolescents: review cardiovascular history and assess for physical signs with specialist referral if indicated • Refer for an echocardiogram if not previously done • Undertake SBE prophylaxis as indicated by findings
Adults: ~ 50% have cardiovascular concerns, commonly acquired mitral valve prolapse (MVP) and valvular regurgitation	☐ Ascertain a comprehensive cardiovascular history ☐ Undertake an annual cardiac exam, with echocardiogram to confirm new abnormal findings and follow-up depending on the type of cardiovascular problem present or refer to an Adult Congenital Heart specialist or Disease clinic ☐ Monitor regularly those that have had surgery in childhood ☐ An echocardiogram is indicated to assess new abnormal physical findings or if unable to assess adequately by physical exam. Consider echocardiogram to establish baseline cardiac anatomy and function if not previously done or records are unavailable [1]
4. RESPIRATORY	
Children and Adults: 50%-80% have obstructive sleep apnea (OSA)	☐ Newborn: Refer to an ENT surgeon if recurring otitis media infections ☐ Treat infections promptly and aggressively
Adults: 50%-80% have obstructive sleep apnea (OSA)	☐ Ascertain a detailed sleep history, with special attention to OSA symptoms. Refer to an ENT surgeon, including sleep study, if OSA is suspected ☐ If aspiration pneumonia is suspected, investigate for possible swallowing disorder and gastro-esophageal reflux disease

CONSIDERATIONS	RECOMMENDATIONS
5. GASTROINTESTINAL	
Children: ~ 50% have gastrointestinal (GI) tract anomalies including duodenal atresia, celiac disease, Hirschsprung disease, and imperforate anus	☐ Newborn: with vomiting or absent stools, check for GI tract blockage and refer to a gastroenterologist ☐ Infants and children: anticipate constipation; treat with fluid/fibre/laxative/stool softener/exercise/dietary change ☐ From 2-3 years of age, screen for celiac disease ☐ Establish good dietary and exercise habits to prevent or manage obesity
Adults: ~ 95% are obese; ~ 7% have celiac disease	☐ Monitor for obesity ☐ Screen for celiac disease, which may present in adulthood; screening tests used are the same as in the general population [2] ☐ Test for *Helicobacter Pylori* and treat if positive, regardless of symptoms ☐ Manage constipation proactively
6. GENITOURINARY	
Children: Cryptorchidism is common	☐ Assess for hypogonadism, undescended testes, and possible testicular germ-cell tumors, or refer to a urologist, as appropriate
Adults: Have increased risk of testicular cancer	☐ Assess annually by clinical exam, and refer to a urologist as appropriate [3]
7. SEXUAL FUNCTION	
Adults: Fertility has been documented in women Fertility in males rarely reported	☐ Counsel regarding fertility possibility and the 50% [4] risk of Down syndrome in offspring
8. MUSCULOSKELETAL (MSK)	
Children: ~15% have atlanto-axial instability (AAI)	☐ Arrange lateral cervical spine X-rays (flexed, neutral, and extended positions) between 3-5 years of age ☐ Screen, as needed, prior to high risk activities (e.g., tumbling) and if participating in Special Olympics ☐ Undertake an annual neurological exam for signs or symptoms of spinal cord compression. If present, refer urgently to a neurosurgeon and arrange an urgent MRI ☐ Obtain a detailed MSK history with particular attention to possible joint subluxations/dislocations, scoliosis, and hip abnormalities
Adults: Continued risk for spinal cord compression secondary to AAI Though data are limited, osteoporosis (associated with increased fractures risk) may be more common in older adults with Down syndrome than in similar aged individuals in the general population or with other developmental disabilities	☐ Undertake an annual neurological exam and assess for evidence of spinal cord compression ☐ Arrange lateral cervical spine X-rays if not previously done, if presenting with signs and symptoms of AAI or if participating in Special Olympics ☐ Take detailed history and attend to joint complaints, scoliosis, and hip abnormalities ☐ If suspected, undertake bone mineral density (BMD) screening and refer to an appropriate specialist if indicated ☐ Encourage ambulation/mobility and weight reduction if obesity is present to decrease the risk of osteoarthritis

CONSIDERATIONS	RECOMMENDATIONS
9. NEUROLOGICAL	
Children: Epilepsy in up to 22%	☐ Take careful neurological history with particular attention to seizures (infantile spasms or tonic-clonic-type) ☐ Arrange an EEG and refer to a neurologist
Adults: Dementia is frequent and occurs earlier: 11%: 40 – 49 y, 77%: 60 – 69 y, Up to 75% with dementia have seizures with frequency increasing with age	☐ Obtain a neuropsychiatric history at every visit with particular attention to change in behaviour, loss of function/activities of daily living, and new onset seizures ☐ If functional decline and/or signs/symptoms of dementia, use history, exam, and blood work to check for other conditions and treatable causes (e.g., hearing/vision deficits, obstructive sleep apnea, hypothyroidism, chronic pain, medication side effects, depression, menopause, low folic acid/vitamin B12) ☐ For possible seizures, arrange an EEG and refer to a neurologist
10. DERMATOLOGICAL	
Children and Adults: Dry skin, atopic dermatitis, seborrheic dermatitis, chelitis, impetigo, and alopecia areata are more common than in general population	☐ Examine skin as part of routine care ☐ Treat as per general population, with referral to dermatologist as needed
11. BEHAVIOURAL/MENTAL HEALTH	
Children: Self-talk is very common; autism spectrum disorder occurs in 5% - 10% of children with DS	☐ Review regularly with respect to behavioural concerns ☐ Review for positive or negative signs suggestive of psychosis
Adults: ~ 30% have a psychiatric disorder, including depression	☐ Review regularly with respect to behavioural concerns ☐ Ascertain neuropsychiatric history at every visit, with particular attention to changes in behaviour, loss of function/activities of daily living, and new onset seizures
12. ENDOCRINE	
Children: ~ 1% have congenital hypothyroidism; ~ 20% develop hypothyroidism after birth	☐ Review neonatal screening ☐ Ascertain TSH and free T4 tests to confirm euthyroid status at 6 and 12 months, then annually ☐ If signs of hyperthyroidism in adolescence, check for autoimmune thyroiditis

CONSIDERATIONS	RECOMMENDATIONS
Adults: 15%-50% are hypothyroid Subclinical hypothyroidism, hyperthyroidism, and autoimmune thyroiditis are more common than in the general population	☐ For adults who are euthyroid, check TSH and free T4 levels at least once every 5 years [5] (some recommend annually) [6] ☐ If subclinical hypothyroidism (i.e., elevated TSH with normal free T4), follow free T4 every 6 months 4 to one year [7] (some recommend treatment if thyroid antibodies are positive) ☐ Consider checking thyroid function whenever there are changes in mental status, behaviour or functional abilities
13. HEMATOLOGICAL	
Children and Adults: Increased frequency of transient myeloproliferative disorder and leukemia No increased risk of leukemia in adults	☐ Neonates to 1 month olds: investigate for polycythemia and thrombocytopenia ☐ Assess history periodically for symptoms of leukemia, with close attention to those with a history of transient myeloproliferative disorder

Resources

22 published Down syndrome health care guidelines were reviewed and compared (For full list of references, see **www.surreyplace.on.ca/Clinical-Programs/Medical-Services/Pages/PrimaryCare.aspx**)

Down syndrome websites that may be helpful for families and caregivers
Canadian Down Syndrome Society **www.cdss.ca/**
Down Syndrome Education International [DownsEd] **www.downsed.org/**
Down Syndrome: Health Issues by Dr. Len Leshin **www.ds-health.com/**
Down Syndrome Medical Interest Group [DSMIG-UK] **www.dsmig.org.uk/**
National Down Syndrome Society [USA] **www.ndss.org/**

Developed by: *Forster-Gibson, Cynthia, MD, PhD* and *Berg, Joseph M, MB, BCh, MSc, FRCPSYCH, FCCMG*

Expert Clinician Reviewers
Thanks to the following clinicians for their review and helpful suggestions.

Brian Chicoine, MD
Medical Director, Adult Down Syndrome Center
of Lutheran General Hospital
Park Ridge, Illinois

Len Leshin, MD
Down Syndrome: Health Issues
Corpus Christi, Texas

References
1. Lin AE, Basson CT, Goldmuntz E, Magoulas PL, McDermott DA, McDonald-McGinn DM, et al. Adults with genetic syndromes and cardiovascular abnormalities: clinical history and management. Genet Med 2008 Jul;10(7):469-94.

2. National Institute for Clinical Excellence [NICE]. Coeliac disease: recognition and assessment of coeliac disease – Quick reference guide. Nice clinical guideline 86. London: National Institute for Clinical Excellence [NICE]; 2009. Available from **www.nice.org.uk/nicemedia/pdf/CG86QuickRefGuide.pdf**.

3. Patja K, Pukkala E, Sund R, Iivanainen M, Kaski M. Cancer incidence of persons with Down syndrome in Finland: a population-based study. Int J Cancer 2006 Apr 1;118(7):1769-72.

4. Galley R. Medical management of the adult patient with Down syndrome. JAAPA. 2005 Apr;18(4):45,6, 48, 51-2.

5. Prasher V, Gomez G. Natural history of thyroid function in adults with Down syndrome--10-year follow-up study. J Intellect Disabil Res 2007 Apr;51(Pt 4):312-7.

6. McGuire D, Chicoine B. Chapter 2: Assessing the physical health/mental health connection. In: McGuire D, Chicoine B, editors. Mental wellness in adults with Down syndrome: A guide to emotional and behavioral strengths and challenges. Bethesda, MD: Woodbine House; 2006. p. 9-28.

7. Wallace RA, Dalton AJ. Clinicians' guide to physical health problems of older adults with Down syndrome. Journal on Developmental Disabilities 2006;12 (1 [Supplement 1]):1-92. Available from **www.oadd.org/publications/journal/issues/vol12no1supp/DS_supplement_1.pdf**.

Health Watch Table — Fragile X Syndrome
Forster-Gibson and Berg 2011

CONSIDERATIONS	RECOMMENDATIONS
1. HEENT (HEAD, EYES, EARS, NOSE, THROAT)	
Children Vision: strabismus, refractive errors are common	☐ Undertake newborn vision and hearing screening and an auditory brainstem response (ABR)
Hearing: recurrent otitis media is common	☐ Refer for a comprehensive ophthalmologic examination by 4 years of age
Nose: sinusitis is common	☐ Visualize tympanic membranes at each visit
Adults: strabismus and refractive errors are common	☐ Undertake hearing and vision screening at each visit with particular attention to myopia and hearing loss
2. DENTAL	
Children and Adults: High arched palate and dental malocclusion are common	☐ Refer to a dentist for an annual exam
3. CARDIOVASCULAR	
Children: Mitral Valve Prolapse (MVP) is less common in children (~10%), but may develop during adolescence	☐ Auscultate for murmurs or clicks at each visit. If present, do an ECG and echocardiogram; refer to cardiologist, if indicated
Adults: MVP is common (~ 80%). Aortic root dilation usually is not progressive Hypertension is common and exacerbated by anxiety	☐ Undertake an annual clinical exam. Based on findings, obtain an ECG and echocardiogram. Refer to cardiologist, as appropriate ☐ Measure BP at each visit and at least annually ☐ Treat hypertension when present
4. RESPIRATORY	
Children & Adults: Obstructive sleep apnea (OSA) may be due to enlarged adenoids, hypotonia or connective tissue dysplasia	☐ Ascertain a sleep history and assess for evidence of OSA ☐ Obtain a sleep study as appropriate
5. GASTROINTESTINAL	
Children: In infants, feeding problems are common with recurrent emesis associated with Gastroesophageal Reflux Disease (GERD) in ~ 30% of infants	☐ Refer for assessment of GERD. Thickened liquids and upright positioning may be sufficient to manage GERD
6. GENITOURINARY	
Children and Adults: Inguinal hernias are relatively common in males Macroorchidism generally develops in late childhood and early adolescence and persists Ureteral reflux may persist into adulthood	☐ Assess for inguinal hernia annually beginning at age 1 year ☐ Macroorchidism can be measured with an orchidometer; reassure parents and patients that it does not require treatment ☐ Evaluate recurring urinary tract infections (UTI) with cystourethrogram and renal ultrasound. Refer to a nephrologist or urologist as needed ☐ Consider and assess for a renal etiology, such as scarring, as the basis for persistent hypertension
7. SEXUAL FUNCTION	
Adults: Males and females are fertile	☐ Consider discussion of recurrence risk and reproductive options as a basis for referral to a geneticist. Make such a referral even if fragile X is only suspected so that molecular testing can be undertaken in the person concerned and relevant family members

CONSIDERATIONS	RECOMMENDATIONS
8. MUSCULOSKELETAL (MSK)	
Children & Adults: Hyperextensible joints and pes planus are common. Scoliosis, clubfeet, joint dislocations (particularly congenital hip) may also occur	☐ Undertake an MSK exam at birth, then every 4 months to adulthood, then at least annually ☐ Elicit a history of possible dislocations ☐ Refer to an orthopedic surgeon as dictated by clinical findings ☐ Referral to an occupational therapist (OT) in childhood is essential ☐ Consider referring to a physiotherapist and podiatrist for orthotics
9. NEUROLOGY	
Children & Adults: ~ 20% have epilepsy (may include generalized tonic-clonic seizures, staring spells, partial motor seizures, and temporal lobe seizures) Hypotonia is common, in addition to fine and gross motor delays Epilepsy occasionally persists into adulthood	☐ Ascertain a history of seizures, which usually present in early childhood ☐ Assess for atypical seizures in adulthood if suspicious findings occur or if intellectual function decreases ☐ Arrange an EEG if epilepsy is suspected from the history ☐ Refer to a neurologist as dictated by clinical findings
10. BEHAVIOURAL/MENTAL HEALTH	
Children: 70% - 80% are hyperactive; ~ 30% have autism Autistic-like features are common and may indicate concurrent Autism Spectrum Disorder Anxiety and mood disorders can also be present Some features of autism, tantrums and aggression as well as anxiety and mood disorders may be treated with specific pharmacological agents Sensory defensiveness is common	☐ Make an early referral to a clinical psychologist for essential parental teaching of appropriate behaviour modification techniques following diagnosis ☐ Encourage use of antioxidants including Vitamin E, Vitamin C, folate and fruit juices ☐ Hyperactivity may be managed using stimulant medications after age 5 years ☐ Refer to an Intensive Behavioural Intervention (IBI) Autism treatment program if Autism Spectrum Disorder is present ☐ Consider a referral to a psychiatrist for possible mental health disorders ☐ Refer to a speech and language therapist following diagnosis ☐ Refer to an occupational therapist (OT) for a sensory diet and sensory integration program
Adults: Aggressive behaviour, sensory defensiveness, Attention Deficit Hyperactivity Disorder (ADHD), mood instability, and anxiety are common in adolescence and adulthood	☐ Consider referral to a psychiatrist or psychologist to assess and manage possible mental health disorders ☐ Violent outbursts are frequent, especially in males, and may respond to behavioural and/or pharmacological measures (as for children)
11. ENDOCRINE	
Children: Precocious puberty may occur	☐ Include attention in clinical examination to signs of precocious puberty in females. Refer to an endocrinologist for consideration of use of a gonadotropin agonist to manage precocious puberty
Adults: Premenstrual symptoms (PMS) may be severe	☐ Ascertain history of PMS with attention to menstruation, anxiety, depression, and mood lability. Consider an SSRI to stabilize mood if PMS symptoms are severe enough

CONSIDERATIONS	RECOMMENDATIONS
12. OTHER	
Occasionally presents as Prader-Willi syndrome-like phenotype	☐ For management of obesity and hyperphagia, consider approaches recommended for persons with Prader-Willi syndrome
PREMUTATION CARRIERS: A late onset tremor/ataxia syndrome has been reported in ~ 40 – 50% of male and ~ 8% of female fragile X premutation carriers	☐ Refer to appropriate specialists (e.g., neurologist, endocrinologist, psychiatrist) as indicated to assist in managing Prader-Willi syndrome-like symptoms
Premature ovarian failure by age 45 has been reported in ~ 20 – 40% of female fragile X premutation carriers	☐ If premutation is suspected but not yet identified, order fragile X DNA testing or refer to a genetics clinic
Psychiatric problems (e.g., mood and anxiety disorders) seem likely to occur in both male and female fragile X premutation carriers [1,2]	☐ To manage depression or anxiety in premutation carriers, SSRIs, regular exercise and counseling have been helpful

Resources

10 published fragile X syndrome health care guidelines reviewed and compared (For full list of references, see **www.surreyplace.on.ca/Clinical-Programs/Medical-Services/Pages/PrimaryCare.aspx**)

Fragile X syndrome websites that may be helpful for families and caregivers

FRAXA Research Foundation **www.fraxa.org**

Fragile X Research Foundation of Canada **www.fragile-x.ca/default2.htm**

The National Fragile X Foundation **www.fragilex.org/html/home.shtml**

Developed by: *Forster-Gibson, Cynthia,* MD, PhD*; Berg, Joseph M,* MB, BCh, MSc, FRCPSYCH, FCCMG

Expert Clinician Reviewers

Thanks to the following clinicians for the review and helpful suggestions.

Randi Hagerman, MD
Medical Director, M.I.N.D Institute
Endowed Chair in Fragile X Research, School of Medicine,
University of California, Davis, California

Carlo Paribello, MD
Director, Fragile X Clinic, Surrey Place Centre, Toronto
President and Medical Director, Fragile X Research Foundation of Canada

References
1. Amiri K, Hagerman RJ, Hagerman PJ. Fragile X-associated tremor/ataxia syndrome: an aging face of the fragile X gene. Arch Neurol 2008 Jan;65(1):19-25.

2. Bourgeois JA, Coffey SM, Rivera SM, Hessl D, Gane LW, Tassone F, et al. A review of fragile X premutation disorders: expanding the psychiatric perspective. J Clin Psychiatry 2009 Jun;70(6):852-62.

Health Watch Table — Prader-Willi Syndrome (PWS)
Forster-Gibson and Berg 2011

CONSIDERATIONS	RECOMMENDATIONS
1. HEENT (HEAD, EYES, EARS, NOSE, THROAT)	
Children: Strabismus and myopia are common	☐ Arrange an auditory brainstem response (ABR) in newborns ☐ Undertake ophthalmology evaluation before 2 years of age, with particular attention to strabismus and visual acuity
Adults: Visual acuity is more commonly diminished than in the general population	☐ Screen vision (DD Guideline 11)[1]
2. DENTAL	
Children: Decreased and sticky saliva flow can predispose to dental caries Delays in teeth eruption and dental overcrowding may occur	☐ Attend to oral hygiene in infants and children including use of soft foam toothbrushes, as well as dental products (toothpaste, sugarless gums, mouthwash) to stimulate saliva production ☐ Arrange regular dental visits with particular attention to crowding of teeth and dental caries ☐ Make orthodontic referral, as necessary
3. CARDIOVASCULAR	
Adults: Cor pulmonale is a commonly reported cardiovascular complication in those who are obese or have significant obstructive sleep apnea (OSA) Cardiopulmonary compromise related to obesity is a common cause of death Hypertension is frequently reported but is uncommon in children	☐ Arrange cardiac evaluation (DD Guideline 13)[1] including cardiology consultation for severely obese patients ☐ Manage underlying obesity (see below)
4. RESPIRATORY	
Children: At risk for sleep disordered breathing Unexpected death may be caused by respiratory obstruction early in Growth Hormone therapy Some tolerate upper respiratory infections poorly	☐ Arrange routine sleep studies during infancy and childhood, and before starting growth hormone therapy and 3 months after initiating it ☐ Ascertain a sleep history and then arrange a sleep study before anesthesia, and if evidence of respiratory distress, sleep apnea, or obesity is present ☐ All children with PWS who have an upper respiratory tract infection should be assessed as soon as possible
Adults: At risk for sleep disordered breathing Cardiopulmonary compromise is the most common cause of death	☐ Ascertain a sleep history with attention to sleep disorders, obesity of any level, snoring, asthma, respiratory infections, and excessive daytime sleepiness ☐ Consider sleep study, respirology, and ENT referral as indicated

CONSIDERATIONS	RECOMMENDATIONS
5. GASTROINTESTINAL AND NUTRITION	
Children: Early concerns include Gastroesophageal Reflux Disease (GERD) and reduced intake due to poor sucking Failure to thrive is common in infancy followed by the development of hyperphagia and obesity in early childhood ~10% develop gall bladder stones Gastric paresis is common	☐ Ascertain a comprehensive GI and nutrition history ☐ Undertake video swallow in neonates based on clinical concerns ☐ Attend to feeding ability and need for assisted feeding ☐ Educate caregivers regarding the necessity of a lower calorie regime, and environmental controls to prevent ready access to food ☐ Attend to diet, nutrition, physical activity, and obesity including plotting weight on standard growth charts ☐ Refer to a dietitian/physician with experience in PWS, if possible, to develop an appropriate nutrition and food security regime ☐ Refer to a gastroenterologist, nutritionist, or dietician as appropriate. Behavioural management programs should be instituted
Adults: Obesity is common without a nutrition and food security program Vomiting often reflects very serious illness (e.g., gastric necropsy) Gastric paresis is common Anal picking is common and may lead to colonic tears/bleeding Constipation due to hypotonia is common	☐ Ascertain a comprehensive GI and nutrition history. Attend to diet, nutrition, and obesity. Refer to a gastroenterologist, dietitian/physician with experience in PWS. Implement the modified Red, Yellow, Green (RYG) [2] diet based on energy requirements (ideally measured by indirect calorimetry) and food security programs ☐ Behavioural management should be maintained with the assistance of a behavioural specialist ☐ In the event of emesis history, the adult with PWS requires immediate evaluation and possibly medical imaging ☐ Provide daily multivitamins ☐ Provide usual interventions to prevent and manage constipation
6. GENITOURINARY	
Children: 80% - 90% of males have cryptorchidism Precocious adrenarche may occur Delayed and incomplete pubertal development is common in both sexes	☐ Verify testicular descent before 2 years of age ☐ Refer to a urologist for cryptorchidism (i.e., absence of one or both testes from the scrotum) ☐ Consider referral to an endocrinologist or gynecologist/urologist, as appropriate, regarding hormone replacement therapy (HRT)
Adults: Incomplete pubertal development is common in both sexes	☐ Refer to gynecologist/urologist, as indicated by clinical findings, and for guidance regarding HRT for both sexes
7. SEXUAL FUNCTION	
Adults: Males and most females are infertile Pregnancy, though unlikely, has been reported	☐ Educate and, if sexually active, counsel ☐ Consider contraception in women who menstruate

CONSIDERATIONS	RECOMMENDATIONS
8. MUSCULOSKELETAL	
Children: 30%-70% have scoliosis ~10% have hip dysplasia Prevention of osteoporosis should start at an early age	☐ Assess for hip dysplasia in early infancy and before 2 years of age ☐ Evaluate for scoliosis from infancy ☐ Monitor with X-rays and refer to an orthopedic surgeon as necessary (Timing of surgical interventions are influenced by the severity of scoliosis and the degree of skeletal maturation) ☐ Ensure adequate intake of calcium and vitamin D from childhood
Adults: Scoliosis and osteopenia/osteoporosis are common in both sexes. Kyphosis may also occur	☐ Screen for scoliosis and kyphosis with spinal X-rays and refer to an orthopedic surgeon as necessary ☐ Assure adequate calcium and vitamin D intake ☐ Screen for osteoporosis with regular Bone Mineral Density tests ☐ Refer to an endocrinologist for consideration of sex-hormone therapy to promote bone health
9. NEUROLOGY	
Children: Hypotonia is common and leads to impaired or absent swallowing and sucking reflexes Hypotonia gradually improves over time Narcolepsy/cataplexy is more common than in general population ~10% have epilepsy	☐ Undertake clinical evaluation with attention to reduced motor activity and psychomotor delay ☐ Consult relevant specialists as indicated by clinical findings ☐ Treat epilepsy as in general population
10. BEHAVIOURAL/MENTAL HEALTH	
Children & Adults: Severe skin picking is common and tends to increase with age Severe maladaptive behaviours are common (including obsessive-compulsive disorders). Psychosis may occur in adolescents and adults. Some features of PWS (e.g., tantrums, aggression, compulsivity, anxiety and mood disorder) may be treated with specific pharmacological agents Risperidone, if indicated, does not usually lead to additional weight gain	☐ Examine skin for evidence of severe skin picking, edema and skin breakdown ☐ Students require a behaviour management program to support their dietary requirements. Avoid food-related occupational and educational activities. Refer to a psychologist or psychiatrist familiar with PWS when necessary to assist in distinguishing between behaviour problems and psychiatric illness

CONSIDERATIONS	RECOMMENDATIONS
11. ENDOCRINE	
Children: Hypothyroidism, diabetes mellitus (Type II), growth hormone (GH) and sex hormone deficiencies may occur GH therapy and strict dietary modifications can normalize body habitus ~ 60% can develop central adrenal insufficiency [3]	☐ Arrange for a PWS pediatric endocrinologist to assess for GH therapy as soon as diagnosis is confirmed. An orthopedic surgery referral may also be indicated before GH treatment is started ☐ Make ENT referral to evaluate upper airway with regards to enlarged tonsils and adenoids prior to starting GH therapy ☐ Screen before and during GH replacement for hypothyroidism, diabetes, and scoliosis (See 4 above for other recommended assessments prior to GH replacement) ☐ Beginning at age 2, assess obese children for diabetes mellitus (Type II) ☐ Refer to an endocrinologist as appropriate for consideration of sex-hormone replacement therapy (See 6 above) ☐ Undertake cortisol evaluation for all children
Adults: As per children, growth and sex hormone deficiencies continue to be found Growth hormone therapy in adults can help to prevent obesity and improve strength and endurance	☐ Undertake clinical assessment with attention to thyroid function, diabetes mellitus (Type II), and hypogonadism ☐ Refer to an endocrinologist, as appropriate, including for consideration of GH and sex-hormone therapy
12. OTHER	
Molecular causes of PWS differ (e.g., in order of frequency: deletion, uniparental disomy, imprinting errors) each of which effect recurrence risks and possible clinical manifestations	☐ Refer to a genetics clinic for evaluation and counseling, where appropriate

Resources

11 published Prader-Willi syndrome health care guidelines reviewed and compared (For full list of references, see **www.surreyplace.on.ca/Clinical-Programs/Medical-Services/Pages/PrimaryCare.aspx**)

Prader-Willi syndrome websites that may be helpful for families and caregivers
Prader-Willi Syndrome Association USA **www.pwsausa.org/**
Prader-Willi Syndrome Network (Ontario) **www.pwsnetwork.ca/pws/index.shtml**
Pittsburgh Partnership, Specialists in Prader-Willi Syndrome **www.pittsburghpartnership.com**

Developed by: ***Forster-Gibson, Cynthia,*** MD, PhD; ***Berg, Joseph M,*** MB, BCH, MSC, FRCPSYCH, FCCMG

Expert Clinician Reviewers
Thanks to the following clinicians for their review and helpful suggestions.

Karen Balko, RD
Coordinator of Prader-Willi Syndrome Clinic, North York General Hospital
Toronto, Ontario

Glenn Berall, MD
Chief of Pediatrics, North York General Hospital
Toronto, Ontario

Suzanne B. Cassidy, MD
Clinical Professor of Pediatrics,
Division of Medical Genetics
University of California, Irvine, California

References

1. Sullivan WF, Berg JM, Bradley E, Cheetham T, Denton R, Heng J, Hennen B, Joyce D, Kelly M, Korossy M, Lunsky Y, McMillan S. Primary care of adults with developmental disabilities: Canadian consensus guidelines. Can Fam Physician 2011;57:541-53.

2. Balko K. Red yellow green: system for weight management. Toronto: Ontario Prader-Willi Syndrome Association; 2005.

3. de Lind van Wijngaarden RF, Otten BJ, Festen DA, Joosten KF, de Jong FH, Sweep FC, et al. High prevalence of central adrenal insufficiency in patients with Prader-Willi syndrome. J Clin Endocrinol Metab. 2008 May;93(5):1649-54.

Health Watch Table — Smith-Magenis Syndrome
Forster-Gibson and Berg 2011

CONSIDERATIONS	RECOMMENDATIONS
1. HEENT (HEAD, EYES, EARS, NOSE, THROAT)	
Children and Adults: Vision: ~ 85% have eye abnormalities, including strabismus, myopia, iris anomalies, and microcornea Retinal detachment, which may be related to self-injurious behaviour in childhood, can occur ~ 25% of adults develop retinal detachment *Hearing:* Chronic ear infections and hearing loss are common *Throat:* Almost all have delayed speech ~ 65% have palatal abnormalities such as velopharyngeal insufficiency (VPI) and cleft palate A deep, hoarse voice is common	☐ Refer to an ophthalmologist following initial diagnosis and annually thereafter ☐ Arrange an annual hearing assessment during childhood then as per DD Guideline 11 [1] ☐ Refer to an ENT surgeon regarding palatal abnormalities following initial diagnosis and annually thereafter ☐ Refer to a speech and language pathologist in early childhood ☐ Consider referring to an occupational therapist (OT) or physiotherapist (PT) regarding oral sensorimotor development
2. DENTAL	
Children and Adults: ~ 75% have dental anomalies including tooth agenesis, premolars and taurodontism	☐ Arrange early and regular dental assessments ☐ Review brushing and flossing techniques with each dental cleaning
3. CARDIOVASCULAR	
Children & Adults: ~ 50% have congenital cardiovascular abnormalities	☐ Obtain an echocardiogram ☐ Refer to a cardiologist at initial diagnosis with follow up arrangements with congenital heart disease clinics, depending on the abnormalities detected. ☐ Follow recommendations for adults as per DD Guideline 13 [1]
4. RESPIRATORY	
Children & Adults: ~ 75% have sleep disturbances usually related to inverted circadian rhythm of melatonin release Melatonin and acebutolol have been used with some success. Over-the-counter melatonin dosages may be inexact and acebutolol use has some contraindications [2]	☐ Undertake a sleep assessment with attention to sleep disturbance, short sleep cycle, early rising, frequent night awakenings, and daytime napping ☐ Consider evening melatonin and morning acebutolol (presumed to counter daytime melatonin release) ☐ Consider strategies to address nighttime safety issues (e.g. enclosed bed) ☐ If there is evidence of obstructive sleep apnea (OSA), arrange a sleep study
5. GASTROINTESTINAL	
Children and Adults: Feeding problems and gastro-esophageal reflux disease (GERD) are common	☐ Undertake a clinical assessment in infancy with attention to feeding problems and evidence of GERD ☐ Monitor regularly for constipation and manage proactively
6. GENITOURINARY	
Children and Adults: Congenital renal or urinary tract abnormalities are common Nocturnal enuresis is common in children	☐ Obtain a renal ultrasound at initial diagnosis ☐ Screen for urinary tract infections with an annual urinalysis or as indicated

CONSIDERATIONS	RECOMMENDATIONS
7. MUSCULOSKELETAL	
Children & Adults: ~ 75% of children develop scoliosis, which tends to become more severe with age	☐ Obtain spine X-rays at diagnosis to assess for vertebral anomalies then annually to assess for scoliosis
8. NEUROLOGY	
Children: ~ 90% have speech and motor delay as well as hypotonia (particularly in infancy) ~ 75% have peripheral neuropathy, often associated with decreased pain sensitivity

Hereditary neuropathy with liability to pressure-related palsies may occur in those with relatively large choromosomal deletions

~ 10%-30% have evident and subclinical epilepsy | ☐ Undertake a neurological assessment at diagnosis and annually thereafter as clinically indicated
☐ Provide periodic neurodevelopmental assessments during infancy and childhood
☐ Arrange speech and language pathologist, PT and OT assessments in infancy and periodically thereafter as appropriate
☐ Consider subclinical seizures if behaviour change occurs
☐ To evaluate seizures, consider electroencephalography (EEG), and Computed Axial Tomography (CAT) scan and Magnetic Resonance Imaging (MRI) scan of head as indicated during infancy and childhood |
| **9. BEHAVIOURAL/MENTAL HEALTH** | |
| *Children & Adults:* Self-injurious, maladaptive, and other behaviours (e.g., head banging, nail yanking, self-hugging, teeth grinding, and inserting objects into body orfices) are nearly always present

These may decrease with time | ☐ In children, arrange early intervention with specific preventative behavioural strategies and special education techniques that emphasize individualized instruction
☐ Use of computer-assisted technology and medication may be helpful
☐ An annual interdisciplinary team assessment of children is warranted and may also be helpful for adults
☐ Plan respite care, family psychological and social supports
☐ Facilitate contact with Parents and Researchers interested in Smith-Magenis Syndrome (PRISMS) to provide support and education (see website below) |
| **10. ENDOCRINE** | |
| *Children and Adults:* ~ 25% are mildly hypothyroid
Hypercholesterolemia is common
Hypoadrenalism, though rare, can occur, particularly in children | ☐ Undertake annual thyroid function and fasting lipid testing
☐ Start screening for hypercholesterolemia in childhood and consider dietary modification for hypercholesterolemia and the possible role of medication
☐ Assess for hypoadrenalism in the event of any serious illness |
| **11. INFECTIOUS DISEASE / IMMUNIZATION** | |
| *Children & Adults:* IgA is reduced in some | ☐ Arrange qualitative immunoglobulin testing at diagnosis
☐ Undertake periodic review if recurrent infections |
| **12. OTHER** | |
| *Children and Adults:* Phenotype/genotype correlations are beginning to emerge for 17p11.2 deletions of different size and for RAI1 mutation carriers

Relatively rare condition, first described in the 1980s, may be under recognized

Limited data and recommendations are currently available for adults but more information is emerging as identified children age | |

Resources

Six published Smith-Magenis syndrome health care guidelines reviewed and compared. (For full list of references see: **www.surreyplace.on.ca/Clinical-Programs/Medical Services/Pages/PrimaryCare.aspx**.)

Smith Magenis syndrome website that may be helpful for families and caregivers **www.prisms.org** is a website for Parents and Researchers interested in Smith-Magenis syndrome or google "PRISMS".

Developed by: ***Forster-Gibson, Cynthia***, *MD, PhD;* ***Berg, Joseph M,*** *MB, BCh, MSc, FRCPSYCH, FCCMG*

Expert Clinician Reviewer
Thanks to the following clinician for her review and helpful suggestions:

Kerry Boyd, MD
McMaster Children's Hospital,
Hamilton Health Sciences, Hamilton, Ontario
Chief Clinical Officer, Bethesda Services, Thorold, Ontario

References

1. Sullivan WF, Berg JM, Bradley E, Cheetham T, Denton R, Heng J, Hennen B, Joyce D, Kelly M, Korossy M, Lunsky Y, McMillan S. Primary care of adults with developmental disabilities: Canadian consensus guidelines. Can Fam Physician 2011;57:541-53.

2. De Leersnyder H, de Blois MC, Bresson JL, Sidi D, Claustrat B, Munnich A. Inversion of the circadian melatonin rhythm in Smith-Magenis syndrome. Rev Neurol (Paris). 2003 Nov;159(11 Suppl):6S21-6.

Health Watch Table — 22q11.2 Deletion Syndrome[a]
Forster-Gibson and Berg 2011

CONSIDERATIONS	RECOMMENDATIONS
1. HEENT (HEAD, EYES, EARS, NOSE, THROAT)	
Children and Adults: ~ 15% have strabismus in addition to other ocular issues (e.g., cataracts, retinal problems) Conductive and/or sensorineural hearing loss (often unilateral) occur in ~ 45% and ~ 10% respectively Most have chronic otitis media There is an increased frequency of velopharyngeal insufficiency (VPI) that is often associated with hyper-nasal speech, some of whom have submucosal cleft palate, and a small minority have overt cleft palate which can lead to nasal regurgitation	☐ Refer to an ophthalmologist for assessment at diagnosis and during preschool years ☐ Refer to an audiologist for evaluation in infancy (or when diagnosed) and every 6 months up to 8 years of age, then annually until adulthood, then according to DD Guideline 11 [1] ☐ Examine the palate in infancy and evaluate for feeding problems and/or nasal regurgitation and, if warranted by clinical findings, refer to a cleft palate team ☐ Refer to a speech and language pathologist for assessment by 1 year of age, sooner if warranted or when diagnosis is made ☐ Evaluate nasal speech quality ☐ Often need regular ear cleaning to remove cerumen
2. DENTAL	
Children and Adults: Retrognathia (over-bite) is common and may cause dental malocclusion Significant dental issues are a recognized part of the syndrome	☐ Refer to a dentist in early childhood ☐ Advocate and ensure for appropriate dental care
3. CARDIOVASCULAR	
Children and Adults: ~ 40% have congenital heart defects, most commonly of the conotruncal type (e.g., Tetralogy of Fallot, Interrupted Aortic Arch, Ventricular Septal Defect)	☐ At the time of diagnosis, complete a cardiovascular assessment, including EKG and echocardiogram ☐ Refer to a cardiologist as warranted by clinical findings
4. RESPIRATORY	
Children: Congenital malformations may lead to upper and/or lower airway obstructions and obstructive sleep apnea (OSA) Most airway concerns resolve spontaneously with time but some require surgical intervention (e.g., Robin sequence)	☐ Refer to an ENT surgeon for evaluation as warranted by clinical findings ☐ Undertake a sleep study in infancy and then as warranted by clinical findings after 3 years of age ☐ Consider a pre-op anesthesia consultation regarding narrow airways prior to the first surgery
Adults: In order of prevalence, there is an increased frequency of recurrent pneumonia, atelectasis, asthma, and chronic obstructive pulmonary disease Those with uncorrected congenital malformations remain at risk for OSA	☐ Consider periodic pulmonary function studies and referral to a respirologist as warranted by clinical findings ☐ Undertake sleep study as warranted by clinical findings

[a] Includes: DiGeorge Syndrome (DGS), Velocardiofacial Syndrome (VCFS), Shprintzen Syndrome, Conotruncal Anomaly Face Syndrome (CTAF), Caylor Cardiofacial Syndrome, and Autosomal Dominant Opitz G/BBB Syndrome

CONSIDERATIONS	RECOMMENDATIONS
5. GASTROINTESTINAL	
Children and Adults: Feeding difficulties, related to pharyngeal and gastrointestinal tract hypotonia, commonly lead to failure to thrive Dysphagia and constipation are common ~ 20% develop gallstones	☐ Refer to a gastroenterologist and feeding specialist (e.g., speech-language pathologist) ☐ Treat constipation ☐ If difficulty swallowing pills, adapt medication regime (e.g., provide with liquid medication, crush pills) ☐ Consider obtaining an abdominal ultrasound in adults to assess for gallstones ☐ Follow DD Guideline 15 [1] for recommendations for managing constipation and Gastroesophageal reflux disease (GERD)
6. GENITOURINARY	
Children and Adults: Up to ~ 33% may have renal tract anomalies ~ 10% may develop renal failure in adulthood	☐ Undertake a renal ultrasound at the time of diagnosis ☐ Maintain surveillance for urinary tract infections (UTIs) ☐ Determine creatinine levels at diagnosis and annually thereafter
7. SEXUAL FUNCTION	
Children and Adults: People with the 22q11.2 deletion syndrome are fertile and have a 50% chance of transmitting the 22q11.2 deletion to children	☐ Referral for genetic counseling may be appropriate
8. MUSCULOSKELETAL	
Children and Adults: Many have skeletal abnormalities, most commonly vertebral or rib anomalies A minority have short stature during childhood which improves by adulthood	☐ Undertake cervical spine X-rays after age 4 years to assess for vertebral anomalies and instability on flexion/extension (five views: flexion, extension, AP, lateral, and open mouth) ☐ Arrange chest X-ray to evaluate for thoracic vertebral anomalies ☐ Provide clinical evaluation for scoliosis at diagnosis, during preschool, and periodically thereafter
9. NEUROLOGICAL	
Children and Adults: Impairments due to reduced muscle tone and motor delay are common in children Seizures are frequently associated with hypocalcemia ~ 40% of adults have recurrent (often hypocalcemic) seizures Cord compression may occur related to skeletal anomalies	☐ Undertake a neuro-developmental assessment of infants with particular attention to reduced muscle tone and motor delay ☐ Refer to a physiotherapist (PT) and/or occupational therapist (OT), as needed ☐ Ascertain history with attention to seizures ☐ Following every seizure, check serum ionized calcium and magnesium ☐ Include EEG examination in evaluation if indicated ☐ Symptoms of cord compression are an indication for an emergent referral to a neurologist or neurosurgeon

CONSIDERATIONS	RECOMMENDATIONS
10. BEHAVIOURAL / MENTAL HEALTH	
Children and Adults: Conditions such as Autism Spectrum Disorder (ASD), Attention Deficit Disorder (ADD), Attention Deficit Hyperactivity Disorder (ADHD), and Obsessive-Compulsive Disorder (OCD) are common Treatable anxiety disorders are common Many of the childhood psychiatric disorders do not necessarily persist, nor do they predict psychiatric illness during adulthood Schizophrenia can become apparent in adolescence and ~ 25% develop schizophrenia or other psychotic disorders in adulthood	☐ Ascertain comprehensive behavioural and mental health history ☐ Refer to a psychiatrist if evidence of ASD, ADD, ADHD, or OCD occurs ☐ Assess for psychiatric illness with attention to changes in behaviour, emotional state and thinking, including hallucinations or delusions and at-risk behaviours (e.g., sexual activity, alcohol/drug use) in teens and adults ☐ Refer to a psychiatrist as warranted by clinical findings ☐ Consider psychiatric assessment at or near puberty with behavioural changes
11. ENDOCRINE	
Children & Adults: ~ 60% have episodic hypocalcemia (often missed when mild or transient) Hypocalcemia is due to hypoparathyroidism in children and adults Long-term calcium supplementation can lead to renal calculi Hypo- and hyperthyroidism have been reported in children and adults ~ 4% have growth hormone deficiency ~ 35% of adults are obese ~ 20% of adults have hypothyroidism ~ 5% of adults have hyperthyroidism	☐ Measure serum ionized calcium concentration in neonates then annually to assess for hypoparathyroidism ☐ Assess calcium levels in infancy, every 3 to 6 months, every 5 years through childhood, and every 1 to 2 years thereafter ☐ Be vigilant regarding risk of hypocalcemia with acute illness and childbirth ☐ All patients should have Vitamin D supplementation; those with documented hypocalcemia and/or relative or absolute hypoparathyroidism may require prescribed hormonal forms supervised by endocrinologist ☐ Refer to an endocrinologist as warranted by clinical and laboratory findings and for initial management of hypocalcemia ☐ Consider densitometry to assess for osteopenia earlier than in general population ☐ Undertake T4 and TSH baseline screening [2] ☐ Treat with standard thyroid replacement or antithyroid therapy where warranted [2] ☐ Monitor growth and growth hormone levels annually and consider endocrinology assessment for poor growth
12. HEMATOLOGY	
Children and Adults: Autoimmune diseases (e.g., thrombocytopenia, juvenile rheumatoid arthritis [JRA], Grave's disease, vitiligo, neutropenia, hemolytic anemia) may be more common than in the general population ~ 10% develop splenomegaly	☐ Monitor with CBC; thyroid function annually or if concerns arise ☐ Investigate arthritis problems for JRA and refer to a rheumatologist as warranted

CONSIDERATIONS	RECOMMENDATIONS

13. INFECTIOUS DISEASE/IMMUNIZATION

Children and Adults:

Congenital thymic aplasia is recognizable in infancy [3]

Immune function may be impaired (although thymic aplasia is rare, thymic hypoplasia is common); improvement in T-cell production occurs over time

~ 75% have chronic middle ear infections (otitis media) and frequent respiratory infections

Irradiated blood products have been used when blood replacement has been necessary

Recurrent upper and lower respiratory tract infections are common in adults

☐ In addition to obtaining a CBC with differential in newborns, consider undertaking flow cytometry. At age 9 to 12 months (prior to live vaccines), assess flow cytometry, immunoglobulins and T-cell function

☐ For infants, minimize exposure to infectious diseases and withhold live vaccines initially. Refer infants to an infectious disease specialist to assess regarding influenza vaccines, CMV-negative irradiated blood products and RSV prophylaxis

☐ Measure absolute lymphocyte count following initial diagnosis and refer to an immunologist if count is low

☐ Evaluate immune status before offering any live vaccines

☐ Treat respiratory and other infections aggressively in children and adults

14. OTHER

Incidence: 1/4000, but more likely higher and many without typical features

Huge variability in level of developmental disability and the number and severity of associated features

IQ: The majority of affected people with 22q11 deletion fall in the high mild to borderline range; moderate to severe rates and average levels of IQ are less common

A selection bias in reported studies may result in over-estimating some prevalence rates

Resources

11 published 22q11.2 deletion syndrome health care guidelines reviewed and compared. (For full list of references see **www.surreyplace.on.ca/Clinical-Programs/Medical Services/Pages/PrimaryCare.aspx)**

22q11.2 Deletion syndrome websites that may be helpful for families and caregivers
www.c22c.org
www.22q.org

Developed by: *Forster-Gibson, Cynthia, MD, PhD;* ***Berg, Joseph M,*** *MB, BCh, MSc, FRCPSYCH, FCCMG*

Expert Clinician Reviewer
Thanks to the following clinician for her review and helpful suggestions:

Anne Bassett, MD
Director, Clinical Genetics Research Program, Centre for Addiction and Mental Health, Toronto
Canada Research Chair, Schizophrenia Genetics

References
1. Sullivan WF, Berg JM, Bradley E, Cheetham T, Denton R, Heng J, Hennen B, Joyce D, Kelly M, Korossy M, Lunsky Y, McMillan S. Primary care of adults with developmental disabilities: Canadian consensus guidelines. Can Fam Physician 2011;57:541-53.

2. Weinzimer SA. Endocrine aspects of the 22q11.2 deletion syndrome. Genet Med 2001 Jan-Feb;3(1):19-22.

3. Bassett AS, Chow EW, Husted J, Weksberg R, Caluseriu O, Webb GD, et al. Clinical features of 78 adults with 22q11 Deletion Syndrome. Am J Med Genet A 2005 Nov 1;138(4):307-13.

SECTION III:
Behavioural and Mental Health Tools

Initial Management of Behavioural Crises in Family Medicine

Consider the crisis behaviour as a **symptom** and not a **disorder**. Behaviour change is often the only way people with developmental disabilities (DD) can express that something is wrong and communicate a need. Very frequently, the "something wrong" is not a psychiatric problem. It may be a signal that the person has a physical health problem causing pain or discomfort or that his/her environment is not an "enabling environment" that meets his/her needs.

Assess and **manage** the behavioural crisis by working with the patient, caregivers and available interdisciplinary team supports.

- Use **Diagnostic Formulation of Behavioural Concerns** to clarify the cause of the behavioural crisis, and assess and manage sequentially any discernible contributing factors, such as medical issues, supports and expectations, emotional issues and psychiatric disorders (see Diagram 1 below).

- **Risk Assessment:** Assess risk to the patient and others.

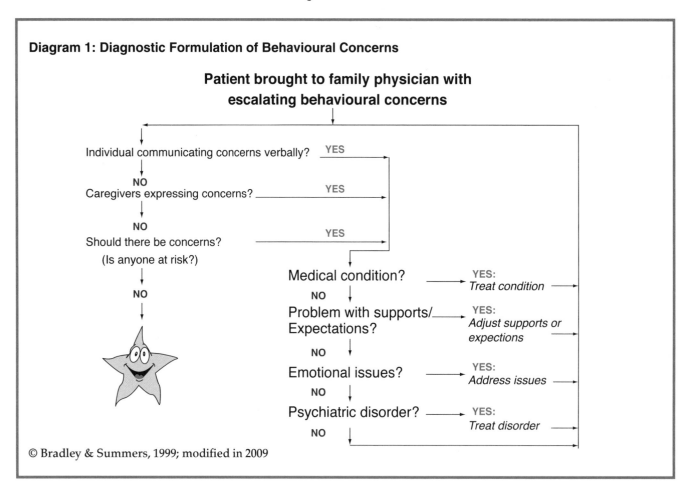

Diagram 1: Diagnostic Formulation of Behavioural Concerns

© Bradley & Summers, 1999; modified in 2009

Note: People with DD are often in a fine balance between their health challenges (physical, emotional and psychiatric) and the available supports and expectations in their environment.

Changes in any of these considerations can upset the balance and precipitate behavioural crises, which signify that help is needed to re-establish or find a better balance. The person may go in and out of crises, until a comprehensive assessment is done, precipitating factors are identified, and a proactive treatment and management plan is initiated.

BEHAVIOURAL CRISIS MANAGEMENT PLAN: FIRST 24 - 72 HOURS

Immediate options to manage risk and escalating or concerning behaviours:

1. **Re-stabilize** the situation in the short term
   Plan, with patient and caregivers, how to re-stabilize the situation and manage the behaviour. These strategies need to reflect the uniqueness of the patient with DD, his/her triggers and coping strategies, helpful environmental changes and modifications, and caregiver resources.
   Consider:
   - What has been helpful or not for this patient with DD in the past.
   - De-escalation strategies:
     – Have patient go to a quiet, safe place (outside the home if indicated)
     – Use existing policies and plans (e.g., agency safety response plans)
   - Increasing environmental supports and/or decreasing environmental stressors:
     – Additional family/agency/staff supports
     – Change in expectations
     – What to do if symptoms worsen or caregivers are unable to manage, including the option of going to an Emergency Department (ED)

2. **Send to Emergency Department**, if indicated:
   - Complete form: *Essential Information for Emergency Department*
   - Information for caregivers: *Guidance about Emergencies for Caregivers*

3. **Use Medications**, if indicated, e.g., PRNs. Consider short-term medication options to stabilize the immediate situation and ensure safety, with a plan for review when the situation stabilizes. See *Rapid Tranquillization of Adults with Crisis Behaviours*.

BEHAVIOURAL MANAGEMENT PLAN: POST-BEHAVIOURAL CRISIS

Plan and manage the underlying problem(s) that *caused or contributed* to the behaviour concerns, in order to meet the needs and enhance the quality of life of the patient with DD, and to prevent recurrences of behavioural crises. See *A Guide to Understanding Behavioural Problems and Emotional Concerns in Adults with Developmental Disabilities*.

Debriefing:
- Schedule an appointment to debrief. Involve the patient with DD, as appropriate, key caregivers, and interdisciplinary team professionals.
  – If a case manager or other needed interdisciplinary resources (e.g., a behaviour therapist) are not in place, access local/regional resources.
- Use/review *Antecedents-Behaviour-Consequences (ABC) Chart* to better understand triggers for behaviours of concern.
- Review crisis strategies, actions taken, and what was effective or ineffective.
- Make recommendations for management and prevention of future behavioural crises. With caregivers and available interdisciplinary resources, begin to develop a comprehensive and proactive *Crisis Prevention and Management Plan* to meet the patient with DD's needs and enhance his/her quality of life.
- For patients who visit the Emergency Department frequently for behavioural causes, it may be helpful to develop a dialogue with local Emergency Department staff.

Review medications: Include regular, PRN, over-the-counter medications, and any possible recreational drugs used. In particular, review any new medications prescribed during behavioural crises.

Risk Assessment Tool for Adults with DD in Behavioural Crisis

Utilize risk assessments applicable to the general population. Take into account how the patient's developmental disabilities (DD) affect both risks and protective factors. Note whether recent changes have occurred in any risk or protective factors.

RISK AREA	Flag all areas where there are risk issues – also consider factors which may protect from harm	
	PATIENT WITH DD – RISK FACTORS	**CAREGIVERS / ENVIRONMENT** *(includes possible protective factors)*
SUICIDE	Is the patient verbalizing suicidal thoughts or intent? Is there evidence of suicidal behaviours, poor judgment or mental illness? Is there a history of suicidal or para-suicidal behaviour? Is the patient not able to identify reasons to keep on living?	Is a means available for the person to commit suicide? Are caregivers unable to supervise and protect the person?
SELF HARM	Is the patient engaging in, or is there evidence of, self harm? Is the patient verbalizing intent to self harm? Does the patient have a history of self harm behaviour?	Are means available for the person to harm self? Are caregivers able to supervise and protect the person?
SELF NEGLECT	Is the patient unable to care for self? Is the patient unwilling to accept support from others? Is there evidence of neglect and behaviours that put the patient at risk?	Are others available and able to assist in the person's care?
VICTIMIZATION OR EXPLOITATION	Is the patient being victimized or exploited? Has the patient been victimized or exploited in the past? Is the patient unable to protect self? Does the patient lack insight into possible dangers of the situation? Has the patient failed to show evidence that he/she would ask for help? Has the patient been unable to get help or protection from others in the past?	Are caregivers able to supervise and protect the person?
RISK TO OTHERS	Is the patient verbalizing intent to harm others? Is the patient making physical gestures about hurting others? Has the patient caused physical harm to others? Does the patient have sufficient mobility and strength to potentially harm others? Does the patient's aggression/harmful behaviour tend to escalate quickly and/or unpredictably?	Are there vulnerable individuals in the setting who cannot protect themselves? Can caregivers recognize cues and intervene safely? Can the person be supervised safely in current setting without caregivers being at risk of harm while trying to prevent harm to others?
RISK TO ENVIRONMENT	Has the patient damaged or attempted to damage property in recent past? If yes, what was the nature and extent of damage? Does the patient have sufficient mobility and strength to be able to cause damage to his/her environment? Does the patient escalate rapidly and/or unpredictably?	Are there caregivers able to recognize the escalation, and intervene effectively? Do caregivers feel comfortable about being able to predict and prevent it?

Developed by: ***Elspeth Bradley***, *Psychiatrist, Surrey Place Centre* and ***Yona Lunsky***, *Psychologist, Centre for Addiction and Mental Health*

Reference
Stein W. Modified sainsbury tool: An initial risk assessment tool for primary care mental health and learning disability services. J Psychiatr Ment Health Nurs 2005 Oct;12(5):620-33.

A Guide to Understanding Behavioural Problems and Emotional Concerns	Name: _____ Gender: ____
in Adults with Developmental Disabilities (DD) for Primary Care Providers and Caregivers	(last, first)

Name: _____ Gender: ____
(last, first)
Address: _____
Tel. No: _____
DOB (dd/mm/yyyy): _____
Health Card Number: _____

This guide is intended for use by primary care providers and, where available, an interdisciplinary team (**Part A**), *with input from patient's caregivers or support persons* (**Part B**). It aims to help identify the causes of behavioural problems, in order to plan for treatment and management, and prevent reoccurrence.

PART A: PRIMARY CARE PROVIDER SECTION

Date (dd/mm/yyyy):	**Presenting Behavioural Concerns:**

Etiology of developmental disability, if known:

Additional disabilities:

☐ Autism spectrum disorder   ☐ Hearing impairment   ☐ Visual impairment   ☐ Physical disability

☐ Other disability (specify): _____   ☐ Previous trauma   ☐ Physical   ☐ Emotional

Family history of: ☐ Medical disorders (specify)
                     ☐ Psychiatric disorders (specify)

What is the patient's most recent level of functioning on formal assessment? Year done: _____

☐ BORDERLINE   ☐ MILD   ☐ MODERATE   ☐ SEVERE   ☐ PROFOUND   ☐ UNKNOWN

DIAGNOSTIC FORMULATION OF BEHAVIOURAL CONCERNS

Patient brought to family physician with escalating behavioural concerns

Individual communicating concerns verbally?   YES

NO
Caregivers expressing concerns?   YES

NO
Should there be concerns?   YES
(Is anyone at risk?)

NO

Medical condition?   YES: *Treat condition*

NO
Problem with supports/ Expectations?   YES: *Adjust supports or expections*

NO
Emotional issues?   YES: *Address issues*

NO
Psychiatric disorder?   YES: *Treat disorder*

NO

© Bradley & Summers 1999; modified in 2009

PART A: PRIMARY CARE PROVIDER SECTION	Name:
	DOB:

1. REVIEW OF POSSIBLE MEDICAL CONDITIONS [See also Preventive Care Checklist]

Many medical conditions present atypically in people with developmental disabilities. In some cases the only indicator of a medical problem may be a change in behaviour or daily functioning. Consider a complete review of systems, a physical exam, and necessary investigations until the cause of the behaviour change is identified.

Would you know if this patient was in pain? ☐ No ☐ Yes: If yes, how does this patient communicate pain?

☐ Expresses verbally ☐ Points to place on body ☐ Expresses through non-specific behaviour disturbance (describe):

☐ Other (specify): _____

Could pain, injury or discomfort (e.g., fracture, tooth abscess, constipation) be contributing to the behaviour change?

☐ No ☐ Yes ☐ Possibly: _____

Assess/Rule out: _____

☐ Medical condition giving rise to physical discomfort (e.g., rash or itch)

☐ Medication side effect

☐ Change in medication   ☐ Dysmenorrhea/Premenstrual syndrome

☐ Allergies   ☐ Peri-menopausal/menopausal (may start earlier)

☐ Vision problem (e.g., cataracts)   ☐ Musculoskeletal (arthritis, joints)

☐ Hearing problem   ☐ Osteoporosis

☐ Dental problem   ☐ Degenerative disc disease (DDD)

☐ Cardiovascular   ☐ Spasticity

☐ Respiratory   ☐ Neurological (e.g., seizures, dementia)

☐ Pneumonia   ☐ Dermatological

☐ GERD/Peptic ulcer disease/*H.pylori* infection   ☐ Sensory discomfort (e.g., new clothes, shoes)

☐ Constipation, or other lower GI problems   ☐ Hypothyroidism

☐ UTI   ☐ Diabetes (I or II)

☐ Sleep problems/sleep apnea

☐ Other: _____

Comments:

2. PROBLEMS WITH ENVIRONMENTAL SUPPORTS OR EXPECTATIONS

Review Caregiver Information   *Identify possible problems with supports or expectations*

☐ **Stress or change in the patient's environment?** (e.g., living situation, day program, family situation)

☐ **Insufficient behavioural supports?**

☐ **Patient's disabilities not adequately assessed or supported?**
(e.g., sensory and communication supports for patients with autism)

☐ **Insufficient staff resources?**
(e.g., to implement treatment, recreational, vocational or leisure programs)

☐ **Inconsistencies in supports and staff approaches?**

☐ **Insufficient training/education of direct care staff?**

☐ **Signs of possible caregiver burnout?** (e.g., negative attitudes towards person, impersonal care, difficult to engage with staff, no or poor follow through in treatment recommendations)

Do caregivers seem to have inappropriate expectations associated with:

Recognizing or adjusting to identified patient needs   ☐ Yes ☐ No ☐ Unsure

Over- or under-estimating patient's abilities (boredom or under-stimulation) ☐ Yes ☐ No ☐ Unsure

Comments:

| PART A: PRIMARY CARE PROVIDER SECTION | Name: |
| | DOB: |

3. REVIEW OF EMOTIONAL ISSUES

Review Caregiver Information   *Identify possible emotional issues*

Summary and comments re emotional issues (e.g., related to change, stress, loss):

4. REVIEW OF POSSIBLE PSYCHIATRIC DISORDERS

History of diagnosed psychiatric disorder: ☐ No   ☐ Yes – Diagnosis: _____

History of admission(s) to psychiatric facility: ☐ No   ☐ Yes *(specify):* _____

(See Appendix: Psychiatric Symptoms and Behaviours Screen)

Summary and comments re symptoms and behaviours indicating possible psychiatric disorder:

SUMMARY OF FACTORS THAT MAY CONTRIBUTE TO BEHAVIOURAL ISSUES

PART A: PRIMARY CARE PROVIDER SECTION	Name: DOB:

MANAGEMENT PLAN: Use the "Diagnostic Formulation of Behavioural Concerns" to assess and treat causative and contributing factors

1. **Physical exam, medical investigations indicated**

2. **Risk assessment**

3. **Medication review**

4. **Referrals for functional assessments and specialized medical assessments as indicated**
   - e.g., to psychologist, speech and language pathologist, occupational therapist for assessments and recommendations re adaptive functioning, communication, sensory needs or sensory diet
   - e.g., genetic assessment/reassessment, psychiatric consult

5. **Assessment and treatment and referral as indicated for**
   - Supports and expectations
   - Emotional issues
   - Psychiatric disorder

6. **Review behavioural strategies currently being used, revise as needed**
   - De-escalation strategies
     – Use of a quiet, safe place
     – Safety response plan
   - Supports
   - Use of "as needed" (PRN) medications

7. **Identify and access local and regional interdisciplinary resources for care of patient**
   - Case management resources
   - Behaviour therapist
   - Other

8. **Focus on behaviours**
   - Identify target symptoms and behaviours to monitor
   - Institute use of *Antecedent-Behaviour-Consequence (ABC) Chart*

9. **Develop a proactive and written Crisis Prevention and Management Plan with caregivers and an interdisciplinary team**
   - Applicable for all environments in which the behaviour could occur, e.g., home, day program or community
   - Caregivers to monitor for triggers of behaviour problems and use early intervention and de-escalation strategies
   - Periodic team collaboration to review issues, plan and revise, as needed
   - If hospital and/or Emergency Department (ED) involved, consider including ED staff in developing the Crisis Prevention and Management Plan

10. **Regular and periodic medication review**
    - Use *Auditing Psychotropic Medication Therapy* tool for review of psychotropic medications

PART B: CAREGIVER SECTION
(Caregiver to fill out or provide information)

Name:

DOB:

What type of Developmental Disability does the patient have (i.e., what caused it?)

(e.g., Down syndrome, fragile X syndrome) _____   ☐ Unsure/don't know

What is the patient's level of functioning?

☐ BORDERLINE   ☐ MILD   ☐ MODERATE   ☐ SEVERE   ☐ PROFOUND   ☐ UNKNOWN

BEHAVIOURAL PROBLEM

When did the behavioural problem start?	When was patient last "at his/her best"? (i.e., before these behaviour problems)
(dd/mm/yyyy) _____	(dd/mm/yyyy) _____

Description of current difficult behaviour(s):

Has this sort of behaviour happened before?

What, in the past, helped or did not help to manage the behaviour?
(include medications or trials of medications to manage behaviour[s])

What is being done now to try to help the patient and manage his/her behaviours? How is it working?

Risk? ☐ To self ☐ To others ☐ To environment	☐ Aggression to others ☐ Self-injurious behaviour	Severity of Damage or Injury ☐ mild (no damage) ☐ moderate (some) ☐ severe (extensive)	Frequency of Distressing (Challenging) Behaviour ☐ more than once daily ☐ daily ☐ weekly ☐ monthly

Please check (√) if there has been any recent deterioration or change in:

☐ mood

☐ bowel/bladder continence

☐ appetite

☐ sleep

☐ social involvement

☐ communication

☐ interest (in leisure activities or work)

☐ seizure frequency

☐ self care (e.g., eating, toileting, dressing, hygiene)

☐ independence

☐ initiative

☐ cognition (e.g., thinking, memory)

☐ movement (standing, walking, coordination)

☐ need for change in supervision and/or placement

When did this change/deterioration start?

Caregiver comments:

PART B: CAREGIVER SECTION (Caregiver to fill out or provide information)	Name: DOB:

DIAGNOSTIC FORMULATION OF BEHAVIOURAL CONCERNS

Patient brought to family physician with escalating behavioural concerns

Individual communicating concerns verbally? — YES

NO
Caregivers expressing concerns? — YES

NO
Should there be concerns?
(Is anyone at risk?)

NO

Medical condition? — YES: *Treat condition*

NO

Problem with supports/ Expectations? — YES: *Adjust supports or expections*

NO

Emotional issues? — YES: *Address issues*

NO

Psychiatric disorder? — YES: *Treat disorder*

NO

© Bradley & Summers 1999; modified in 2009

1. POSSIBLE PHYSICAL HEALTH PROBLEMS OR PAIN

Are you or other caregivers aware of any **physical health or medical problems** that might be contributing to the patient's behaviour problems? ☐ No ☐ Yes: If yes, please specify or describe:

Could pain, injury or discomfort be contributing to the behaviour change? ☐ No ☐ Yes ☐ Possibly
Specify: _____

Would you know if this patient was in pain? ☐ No ☐ Yes: How does this patient communicate pain?

☐ Expresses verbally ☐ Points to place on body

☐ Expresses through non-specific behaviour disturbance (describe): _____

☐ Other (specify): _____

Are there any concerns about medications or possible medication side effects?

2.1: CHANGES IN ENVIRONMENT *before* problem behaviour(s) began

Have there been any recent changes or stressful circumstances in:

☐ **Caregivers?** (family members, paid staff, volunteers)

☐ **Care provision?** (e.g., new program or delivered differently, fewer staff to support)

☐ **Living environment?** (e.g., co-residents)

☐ **School or day program?**

PART B: CAREGIVER SECTION	Name:
	DOB:

2.2: SUPPORT ISSUES

Are there any problems in this patient's support system that may contribute to his/her basic needs not being met?

Does this patient have a ☐ **hearing** or ☐ **vision problem?** ☐ No ☐ Yes: If yes, what is in place to help him/her?

Does this patient have a **communication problem?** ☐ No ☐ Yes: If yes, what is in place to help him/her?

Does this patient have a problem with **sensory triggers?** ☐ No ☐ Yes: If yes, what is in place to help him/her?
⇒ *If yes*, do you think this patient's environment is ☐ over-stimulating? ☐ under-stimulating? or ☐ just right for this patient?

Does environment seem **too physically demanding** for this patient? ☐ No ☐ Yes

Does this patient have enough opportunities for **appropriate physical activities?** ☐ No ☐ Yes

Does this patient have **mobility problems** or **physical restrictions?** ☐ No ☐ Yes: If yes, what is in place to help him/her? If yes, does he/she receive physiotherapy?

Are there **any supports or programs that might help this patient** and which are not presently in place**?**
☐ No ☐ Yes: If yes, please describe:

Caregiver comments:

3: EMOTIONAL ISSUES   Please check (√) if any of these factors may be affecting this patient:

Any recent change in relationships with significant others
(e.g., staff, family, friends, romantic partner)
☐ **Additions** (e.g., new roommate, birth of sibling)
☐ **Losses** (e.g., staff change, housemate change)
☐ **Separations** (e.g., decreased visits by
   volunteers, sibling moved out)
☐ **Deaths** (e.g., parent, housemate, caregiver)

Issues of assault or abuse

	Past	Ongoing	Date(s)
☐ Physical	☐	☐	_____
☐ Sexual	☐	☐	_____
☐ Emotional	☐	☐	_____
☐ Exploitation	☐	☐	_____

Comments:

☐ **Teasing or bullying**
☐ **Anxiety about completing tasks**
☐ **Issues regarding sexuality and relationships**
☐ **Being left out of an activity or group**
☐ **Stress or upsetting event, at school or work**
☐ **Inability to verbalize feelings**
☐ **Disappointment(s)**
(e.g., being surpassed by siblings; not being able to meet goals, such as driving or having a romantic relationship)
☐ **Growing insight into disabilities and impact on own life**
(e.g., that he/she will never have children, sibling has boy/girlfriend)
☐ **Life transitions** (e.g., moving out of family home, leaving school, puberty)
☐ **Other triggers** (e.g., anniversaries, holidays, environmental, associated with past trauma)
   Specify:

Caregiver Comments:

| PART B: CAREGIVER SECTION | Name: |
| | DOB: |

Has this patient ever been diagnosed with a psychiatric disorder? ☐ No ☐ Unsure

☐ Yes: _____

Has this patient ever been hospitalized for a psychiatric reason? ☐ No ☐ Unsure

☐ Yes: _____

CAREGIVER CONCERNS AND INFORMATION NEEDS

Do you, and other caregivers, have the information you need to help this patient, in terms of:

- The type of developmental disability the patient has and possible causes of it? ☐ Yes ☐ No ☐ Unsure

- What the patient's abilities, support needs, and potential are? ☐ Yes ☐ No ☐ Unsure

- Possible physical health problems with this kind of disability? ☐ Yes ☐ No ☐ Unsure

- Possible mental health problems and support needs with this kind of disability (e.g., anxiety more common with fragile X syndrome)? ☐ Yes ☐ No ☐ Unsure

- How to help if the patient has behaviour problems/emotional issues? ☐ Yes ☐ No ☐ Unsure

- Recent changes or deterioration in the patient's abilities? ☐ Yes ☐ No ☐ Unsure

Are there any issues of **caregiver stress** or potential burnout? ☐ Yes ☐ No ☐ Unsure

Caregiver comments:

Caregiver's additional general comments or concerns:

Thank you *for the information you have provided. It will be helpful in understanding this patient better and planning and providing health care for him or her.*

PRIMARY CARE PROVIDERS AND CAREGIVERS: Psychiatric Symptoms and Behaviours Screen	Name: DOB:		
Can be filled out by **primary care provider**, or by **caregiver, and reviewed** by primary care provider.			
Symptoms and behaviours	**BASELINE** [1] Check if usually present	**NEW** Check if recent onset	**COMMENTS** If new onset or increased
Anxiety-related			
Anxiety			
Panic			
Phobias			
Obsessive thoughts			
Compulsive behaviours			
Rituals/routines			
Other			
Mood-related			
Agitation			
Irritability			
Aggression			
Self-harm behaviour			
Depressed mood			
Loss of interest Unhappy/miserable Under-activity			
Sleep			
Eating pattern			
Appetite			
Weight (provide details)			
Elevated mood			
Intrusiveness			
Hypersexuality			
Other			
Psychotic-related [2]			
Psychotic and psychotic-like symptoms (e.g., self talk, delusions, hallucinations)			
Movement-related			
Catatonia ('stuck')			
Tics			
Stereotypies (repetitive movements or utterances)			
ADHD-related or Mood Disorder			
Inattention			
Hyperactivity			
Impulsivity			
Dementia-related			
Concentration			
Memory			
Other			
Other			
Alcohol misuse			
Drug abuse			
Sexual issues/problems			
Psychosomatic complaints			

[1] Establish usual baseline i.e., behaviours and daily functioning before onset of concerns.
[2] **Use caution when interpreting psychotic-like symptoms and behaviours** in patients with DD. These may be associated with anxiety (or other circumstances) rather than a psychotic disorder.

ABC (Antecedent-Behaviour-Consequence) Chart

To record baseline information for incongruent, challenging or problematic behaviours*

Name:

DOB:

Occasion Date Time Observer	Pre-existing conditions Factors that increase vulnerability or sensitivity to triggers	Antecedent What happened just before the behaviour occurred and might have triggered it? Include SETTING & ACTIVITY	Behaviour Describe the behaviour as accurately and specifically as possible. Include <u>frequency</u>, <u>duration</u>, and <u>intensity on a scale of 1 to 5 (5 is most severe)</u>.	Consequence Things that happened immediately after the behaviour occurs, and make it more or less likely to happen again
Example				
Date Feb 6/10 **Time** 6:30-7:10 pm **Observer** Rene – primary staff member	John's mother was in hospital with broken hip, and could not visit. John had a toothache. John's usual primary staff member was on holidays.	John was eating supper in kitchen when another resident bumped into him when passing food.	John started to yell and threw his plate across the table. He ran out of room, screamed for 10 minutes and threw cushions around living room. The intensity was 4/5.	Staff tried to direct John to his room for a time-out but he became more agitated. They also tried to distract him with ice cream but were unsuccessful. They directed other residents to leave the room. John began to hit staff when they approached him. Staff observed him from a distance, gave him time and reduced stimuli, and he calmed down in about 30 min.
Date **Time** **Observer**				
Date **Time** **Observer**				
Date **Time** **Observer**				

*Adapted from **www.peatni.org/directory/resources/index.asp** with input from **Caroll Drummond**, Behaviour Therapist, Surrey Place Centre

Crisis Prevention and Management Plan
for Adults with Developmental Disabilities (DD) at Risk of or During a Behavioural Crisis

Consider escalating behaviour problems as symptoms and not as disorders in themselves. Escalating behaviour problems that build to a crisis may be the best or only way that a person with DD can communicate his/her needs and that something is bothering him/her.
Understanding what is underlying the behaviour problems is the key to preventing and managing these problems.

When a person with DD has already experienced a behavioural crisis and there is a risk of recurrence, **debrief** and **develop** a *Crisis Prevention and Management Plan.*

1. *Debrief* after the behavioural crisis with the person with DD, caregivers, and team. Identify what may have contributed to or caused the crisis, and which interventions used were effective or ineffective. Make recommendations regarding preventing and managing possible future crises.
   - **Identify and treat the underlying condition**s that caused or contributed to the crisis behaviours.
   - **Review medications**, particularly psychotropics, and any medication changes made in the Emergency Department (ED).

2. *Develop the Crisis Prevention and Management Plan*
   - **A case manager or behaviour therapist** is often the most appropriate person to coordinate the care planning meeting and to take the lead in developing the *Crisis Prevention and Management Plan*. If there is no case manager in place:
     – Contact the local office of the Ministry of Community and Social Services (MCSS).
     – For patients with Dual Diagnoses (i.e., developmental disabilities and a possible or diagnosed mental health problem), contact the regional Community Network of Specialized Care (CNSC) to request a case manager.
   - Meet as a team with the patient with DD, appropriate caregivers, and interdisciplinary team (e.g., residential caregivers, psychiatrist, nurse, behaviour therapist, service coordinator). If indicated, include Emergency Services (ED, police, ambulance services).
   - Inclusion of the person with DD and caregivers in development of the plan will help to promote consistency in responses to escalating behaviour problems, and will provide a shared way to document stages of escalation for treatment and evaluation.
   - **In the first column** (page 80), identify what the patient's behaviour looks like at each stage. Identify signs of escalation to Stage B (Escalation Stage) and Stage C (Crisis Stage). Early identification of signs of anxiety or agitation provides opportunities for prompt interventions to keep the patient and others in the environment safe and, if possible, to prevent the situation from reaching a crisis.
   - **In the second column** (page 80), identify usually successful de-escalation or intervention strategies that caregivers can use for the given stage. Include when to use them, for how long, how often, and where to record them.
     – Clearly identify when to administer "as needed" (PRN) medication.
     – Clearly identify the circumstances under which the patient should be taken to the ED.
   - Identify the care provider most responsible for regularly reviewing and updating the *Crisis Prevention and Management Plan*.
   - Develop a schedule with the patient and caregivers from all environments for a regular, patient-centred review of the individual and his/her needs, the behaviour problems, the escalation continuum, and corresponding interventions.

Crisis Prevention and Management Plan
Overview – Escalation Stages and Recommended Interventions for Agitated or Aggressive Patients with Developmental Disabilities [1]

Stage	Intervention
A: Prevention: Anxiety or Agitation	Ensure safety of patient and staff. Strengthen environmental supports, decrease stressors.
B: Escalation: Defensive/Verbal Threats	Be Directive - Verbal de-escalation and modelling As above, modify environment to meet patient's needs and ensure safety for everyone.
C: Crisis: Acting Out/Overt Aggression	Crisis Intervention and Safety Strategies: • Continue attempts at verbal de-escalation. • Use physical interventions. • Get PRN medication if ordered and indicated. • Consider calling for help or calling 9-1-1.
R: Post-Crisis Calming: Crisis Resolution	Support patient's return to normal behaviour and activities. Document, and debrief with patient, caregivers, team.

Management of crises and abnormal behaviour may be different for patients with DD than for patients in the general population.

- Patients with DD may behave atypically or unpredictably. For example, attempts to de-escalate the situation verbally may worsen the patient's agitation.
- Approaches to interviewing adapted to patients with DD generally help to engage them and avoid further escalation. (See *Communicating Effectively with People with Developmental Disabilities*.)
- At each stage of your interaction with the patient with DD, make use of the caregivers' knowledge and experience of this individual. Caregivers often have a protocol and recommendations for managing out-of-control behaviour, and protocols may be uniquely tailored to specific individuals. Ask about these and apply them if this can be done safely.

Overview of Behaviours and Recommended Responses ➡ P.79

Template: Crisis Prevention and Management Plan ➡ P.80

Example of completed Crisis Prevention and Management Plan ➡ P.81

See also:
- *Initial Management of Behavioural Crises in Family Medicine*
- *A Guide to Understanding Behavioural Problems and Emotional Concerns in Adults with Developmental Disabilities*
- *Communicating Effectively with People with Developmental Disabilities (DD)*

---

[1] Bradley E, Lofchy J. Learning disability in the accident and emergency department. Advances in Psychiatric Treatment 2005, 11:45-57.

Crisis Prevention and Management Plan [2]
Overview of Behaviour Stages and Recommended Responses

Stage of Patient Behaviour	Recommended Caregiver Responses
Normal, calm behaviour	**Use positive approaches, encourage usual routines** • Structure, routines • Programs, conversation, activities, antecedent interventions, reinforcement
Stage A: Prevention *(Identify early warning signs that signal increasing stress or anxiety.)* Anxiety may be shown in energy changes, verbal or conversational changes, fidgeting, sudden changes in affect, attempting to draw people into a power struggle.	**Be supportive, modify environment to meet needs** • Encourage talking, be empathetic, use a non-judgemental approach, be supportive, increase positive feedback, offer choices. • Use calming object or usual calming approach (e.g., deep breathing) • Use distraction and environmental accommodation (e.g., ↓ noise stimuli, ↑ personal space).
Stage B: Escalation *(Identify signs the patient with DD is escalating into possible behavioural crisis.)* Increasing resistance to requests, refusal, questioning, challenging, change in tone and volume of voice, sense of loss of control, increasing physical activity, loud self talk, swearing to self.	**Be directive** (use verbal direction and modelling), **continue to modify environment to meet needs, ensure safety** • Use verbal intervention techniques, set limits, remember distance. Use visual aids if helpful. • Reassure, discuss past successes, show understanding. • Describe what you see, not your interpretation of it. • If the patient with DD is able to communicate verbally, identify his/her major feeling state (angry, frustrated, anxious), provide answers to questions, generate discussion, state facts, ask short clear questions. • For a non-verbal patient with DD, adjust responses to him/her.
Stage C: Crisis *(Risk of harm to self, others, or environment, or seriously disruptive behaviour, e.g., acting out.)* Verbal threats of aggression, or aggression: • Swearing at people • Explosive, threatening • Using threatening gestures to others or self Physical aggression to self or others: • Hurting self • Kicking, hitting, scratching, choking • Using objects to hurt self or others	**Use safety strategies** • Ensure your own safety, safety of others, and safety of individual. • Use personal space and supportive stance. • Remove potentially harmful objects. • Use clear, short, calm and slow statements. • Remind the patient with DD of pre-established boundaries; remind him/her about the consequences of his/her behaviour but do not threaten him/her. • Get assistance to keep safe. **Use crisis response strategies** Everyone should agree on a plan for what happens at the time of a crisis and the follow-up. For example: • Phone 9-1-1 • In Toronto: call the Mobile Crisis Unit 416-289-2434 • Have caregiver accompany distressed patient to Emergency **Take the patient to ED with the following:** • List of medications from pharmacy • Essential information for Emergency Department • Crisis Prevention and Management Plan
Stage R: Post-crisis resolution and calming • Stress and tension decrease • Decrease in physical and emotional energy • Regains control of behaviour	**Re-establish routines and re-establish rapport** • Attempt to re-establish communication and return to "calm" and normal routines.

---

[2] Based on *Nonviolent Crisis Intervention* ® Training (NVCI) from Crisis Prevention Institute – **www.crisisprevention.com**
• Staff working in agencies serving persons with Developmental Disabilities must be trained, and re-certified annually in NVCI
• Input provided by Caroll Drummond, Behaviour Therapist, Surrey Place Centre

Crisis Prevention and Management Plan [3]
for Adults with Developmental Disabilities (DD) at Risk of or During Behavioural Crises

A Crisis Prevention and Management Plan for an adult patient with DD addresses serious behaviour problems and helps prevent, or prepare for, a crisis. It describes how to recognize the patient with DD's pattern of escalating behaviours. It identifies responses that are usually effective for this patient to prevent (if possible) a behavioural crisis, or to manage it when it occurs. The Crisis Prevention and Management Plan is best developed by an interdisciplinary team.

- Describe stage-specific signs of behaviour escalation and recommended responses.
- Identify when to use "as needed" (PRN) medication.
- Identify under what circumstances the patient with DD should go to the Emergency Department (ED).

Crisis Plan for: _____ **DOB:** _____ **Date** _____

Problem behaviour: _____

Stage of Patient Behaviour	Recommended Caregiver Responses
Normal, calm behaviour	**Use positive approaches, encourage usual routines**
Stage A: Prevention *(Identify early warning signs that signal increasing stress or anxiety.)*	**Be supportive, modify environment to meet needs** *(Identify de-escalation strategies that are helpful for this patient with DD).*
Stage B: Escalation *(Identify signs of the patient with DD escalating to a possible behavioural crisis.)*	**Be directive** (use verbal direction and modelling), **continue to modify environment to meet needs, ensure safety**
Stage C: Crisis *(Risk of harm to self, others, or environment, or seriously disruptive behaviour, e.g., acting out.)*	**Use safety and crisis response strategies**
Stage R: Post-crisis resolution and calming	**Re-establish routines and re-establish rapport**

Individual responsible for coordinating debriefing after any significant crisis, and for regularly updating the Crisis Plan:

Name: _____ **Tel. #:** _____
Name, Designation, Agency

---

[3] See next page for example of completed Crisis Prevention and Management Plan

Example of Completed Crisis Plan

A Crisis Prevention and Management Plan for an adult patient with DD addresses serious problem behaviours and helps prevent, or prepare for, a crisis It describes how to recognize the patient with DD's pattern of escalating behaviours. It identifies responses that are usually effective for this patient to prevent (if possible) a behavioural crisis, or to manage it when it occurs. The Crisis Prevention and Management Plan is best developed by an interdisciplinary team.

- Describe stage-specific signs of behaviour escalation and recommended responses.
- Identify when to use "as needed" (PRN) medication.
- Identify under what circumstances the patient with DD should go to the Emergency Department (ED).

Crisis Plan for: Jack Doe   **DOB:** February 20, 1952   **Date:** May 13, 2010

Problem behaviour: Verbal threats, swearing, physical aggression

Stage of Patient Behaviour	Recommended Caregiver Responses
Normal, calm behaviour Talks well about work, people, follows routine, enjoys others, laughs, good rapport with peers. Prefers quiet, dislikes loud noises from radio, TV.	**Use positive approaches, encourage usual routines** Positive instructions (when you do… then you can…); joke with Jack; clear directions; reinforcement for pleasant conversation about work, others; following routine; being proud of himself.
Stage A: Prevention *(Identify early warning signs that signal increasing stress or anxiety.)* • Complaining about work or co-worker or anyone he has had contact with on arrival at the group home. • Says that they shouldn't be able to do that or they didn't follow the rules.	**Be supportive, modify environment to meet needs** 1. Take Jack to quiet room. Talk with him about what is wrong. (What happened? How does he feel? Illness?) 2. Ask him to develop a solution – what will make it better? (with your help if necessary). 3. Have him write down the problem and solution for later reference when he thinks about it again. *Continue to redirect verbally with positive words.* 4. Reinforce any calm behaviours. *Go to next stage* if behaviour escalates.
Stage B: Escalation *(Identify signs the patient with DD is escalating to possible behavioural crisis.)* • Swearing about people or situations in a loud voice and pacing (walking back and forth from one end of the living room or hallway to the other without stopping).	**Be directive** (use verbal direction and modelling), **continue to modify environment to meet needs, ensure safety** 1. Ask Jack to sit, sit with him (remember distance). 2. Ask to help him discuss or read the solution he wrote earlier. 3. Ask if there is another problem. Resolve. 4. Have him engage in relaxation techniques, e.g., breathing slowly with you. If he refuses to comply, follow direction or escalates, go to *next stage*.
	***PRN: Administer the PRN if Jack swears and paces for five continuous minutes (Stage B) or refuses to calm down and breathe slowly with staff member (Stage C) after two requests.**
Stage C: Crisis *(Risk of harm to self, others, or environment, or seriously disruptive behaviour, e.g., acting out.)* • Throwing objects at the walls or floors. • Jack's pacing becomes quicker and he begins to dart toward things, grabs them and throws them. • Threatening bodily harm and hitting/ kicking others and saying demeaning words or swearing (e.g., "Get out of my way you _____ or I'll hit you.")	**Use safety and crisis response strategies** 1. Keep critical distance. Put something between you and Jack; ensure you have an exit. 2. Say "Stop, Jack, time to calm down, breathe with me" (model breathing). If no reduction/refusal, say, "Jack, stop, I'm calling people to help." 3. Remove or tell others to leave the area. 4. Leave the area – call *9-1-1*. 5. Have patient taken to ED by ambulance, with *Essential Information for ED, Crisis Prevention and Management Plan, list of medications being taken*, and accompanied by a staff member.
Stage R: Post-crisis resolution, calming Jack will go to his own room and talk quietly. He will ask politely if he can talk about what happened when he is calm.	**Re-establish routines and re-establish rapport** When Jack has calmed, talk with him for a few minutes and have him re-engage in his routine as soon as possible. Reinforce Jack's calm activity.

Individual responsible for coordinating debriefing after any significant crisis, and for regularly updating the Crisis Plan:

Name: Michael Smith, Behaviour Therapist, Smalltown Regional Services   **Tel. #:** 705 123 4567

Name, Designation, Agency

* In this example a PRN medication had been prescribed. Team and patient agreed on the circumstances and stage of escalation when it should be given. A line was drawn across this chart to make clear to everyone at what stage of escalation to give the PRN.

Essential Information for Emergency Department (ED)

Name: _____ Gender: _____
(last, first)

Address: _____

Tel. No: _____

DOB (dd/mm/yyyy): _____

Health Card Number: _____

CLIENT INFORMATION
Prefers to be called:

Lives with: ☐ Family ☐ Group home ☐ Foster home
☐ Independent ☐ Other

EMERGENCY CONTACT INFORMATION:

Name:	Relationship:
Tel #: Home: Work or cell:	*Substitute Decision Maker* ☐ Yes ☐ No

HEALTH AND SOCIAL AGENCY CARE PROVIDERS:

Family Physician:	Tel. #:
Psychiatrist:	Tel. #:
Case Manager:	Agency:
Name:	Tel. #:
Preferred hospital / treatment centre:	
Other agencies involved, contact person's name	Tel. #:

REASON FOR REFERRAL TO ED: Safety risks to self, others or environment? ☐ **No** ☐ **Yes** (specify):
_____
_____

BRIEF OVERVIEW OF HEALTH STATUS: Include diagnoses, allergies, etiology of developmental disability (DD) & level of functioning, health issues and risks – physical and behavioural or mental health
_____
_____
_____
_____

Special needs: _____

NB: ATTACH LIST OF CURRENT MEDICATIONS ☐ attached

Copy of Medication Administration Record (MAR) or List from Pharmacy, and send or bring medications

Signature: _____ Date: _____
Print Name, Designation   dd/mm/yyyy

Best contact #: _____

Guidance About Emergencies for Caregivers

ATTEND TO SAFETY ISSUES How can the person in crisis, staff, other residents and the environment be kept safe?	• Use existing successful strategies to manage escalating behaviours • Can the person with developmental disabilities (DD) be safely contained in a quiet, safe place? • What changes can be made in his/her environment to make him/her, other people, and the environment safe? • Is there "as needed" or PRN medication that generally helps the person, and that can safely be given? • Physical restraint is against policy, and not a legal option in group homes
KEEP IN MIND	• *Person with DD and caregiver preferences in decision-making process* • *Attend to uniqueness of the person with DD*
POINT OUT	• Any possible medical symptoms that family/staff may have noticed, for Emergency Medical Services (EMS) and Emergency Department (ED) staff • How the person typically communicates pain and distress

IF SENDING THE PERSON WITH DD TO EMERGENCY DEPARTMENT OR CALLING 911:

• Complete and send *Essential Information for Emergency Department (ED)*

• Attach list of all **current medications** from Medication Administration Record (MAR) or pharmacy list and *bring medications*

• **If PRN medication** is already part or the behavioural management, consider whether an **additional PRN** would assist the person with DD prior to going to the ED

• Consider bringing photos or video showing how this person acts when calm and not calm

WHEN CONTACTING 911

• Explain that the person has a developmental disability
• Alert EMS staff to any special needs, for example:
  – Best way to communicate
  – Importance of caregiver presence to help the person feel safe and comfortable
  – Sensitivity to sensory issues (e.g., noise, lights, textures, personal space)
  – Sensitivity to restraints
  – Reaction of the person with DD to uniformed police, and other people in uniforms or strangers

PATIENT COMFORT PACKAGE FOR ED/HOSPITAL VISITS

Encourage patient/caregivers to bring:
• Comforters (e.g., security blanket, stuffed animal, favourite book, photos)
• Favourite food/drink and snacks (the wait can be long and food may be limited)
• Communication strategies that work (communication aids)
• Someone who knows the person well and knows how hospitals work
• Ways (e.g., photos - video/digital) to illustrate what the person with DD is usually like
• Explanation about how hospitals work (social story appropriate for the person's developmental level)

Bring all medications for the next 12 hours *as ED will not dispense regular medications.*

Developed by: *Yona Lunsky, Psychologist, Centre for Addiction and Mental Health*

Psychotropic Medication Issues
in Adults with Developmental Disabilities (DD)

Overview

Primary care of adults with developmental disabilities: Canadian consensus guidelines (2001) addresses several issues related to psychotropic medication use in this population.

- **Guideline 22** points out that antipsychotic drugs should no longer be regarded as an acceptable routine treatment for problem behaviours.

- **Guideline 26** stipulates that interventions other than medications are usually effective for preventing or alleviating problem behaviours.

- **Guideline 27** notes that psychotropic medications may be problematic for adults with DD and therefore should be used judiciously. Patients may be on multiple medications and thus be at increased risk of adverse medication interactions. Some adults with DD may have atypical responses or side effects at lower doses. Some cannot describe harmful or distressing side effects of the medications they are taking. This Guideline advocates a "start low, go slow" approach in initiating, increasing or decreasing psychotropic medications, and review every three months.

- **Guideline 28** clarifies that antipsychotic medications should not be prescribed as routine treatments of problem behaviours in adults with DD without a robust diagnosis of a psychotic illness.

- **Guideline 29** addresses behavioural crises and identifies circumstances in which psychotropic medications may be used temporarily to ensure safety. Debriefing with caregivers and review of crisis events and response (including medications) after the crisis is recommended to minimize the likelihood of their recurrence.

1. **Recommendations for use of medications for behaviour problems outside of a behavioural crisis, for adults with DD** (Deb 2009, Banks 2008):

   - The goal is not to treat the behaviour per se but to identify the underlying cause of the behaviour disturbance and treat that.

   - Identifying the underlying cause often requires an interdisciplinary team approach.

   - Where the cause of the behaviour remains elusive, despite thorough investigation for medical conditions, environmental contributors to the behaviours of concern, emotional issues or psychiatric disorders, consideration may be given to a trial of medication appropriate to the patient's symptoms.

   - Medication trials should be targeted against specific symptoms (e.g., irritable mood) or behaviours (e.g., incidents of self injury), time limited, and monitored carefully for effectiveness and side effects.

2. Using psychotropic medication for adults with DD (Bradley 1999)

2.1 These medications are used:

- to treat psychiatric illness or disorders. First establish the diagnosis and then treat the illness/disorder according to best practices.

- on a trial basis for psychiatric symptoms and behaviours for which the cause has not yet been identified after a full interdisciplinary assessment.

2.2 Before prescribing, identify symptoms and behaviours that represent a change from usual characteristics for that individual. These may be the behavioural correlates of a psychiatric disorder (e.g., changes in sleep, eating patterns, aggression, non-compliance, regression in skills, or incontinence might indicate a mood disorder).

2.3 Target symptoms and behaviours:

- Identified "target" symptoms and behaviours should be monitored daily by caregivers in the individual's residential and day settings.

- Target symptoms and behaviours are core to the clinical hypothesis as to the psychiatric diagnosis and cause of the mental health concerns (e.g., depressive episode following relocation) and are the criteria against which treatment response should be evaluated.

2.4 Monitoring tools that may be adapted easily to primary care practices include:

- *Antecedent-Behaviour-Consequence (ABC) Charts* to document acute behavioural incidents.

- 24-hour, weekly, and monthly charts to monitor sleep, mood and other behaviours.

- Likert scale charts (with operationally described behaviours on a scale of 0 to 5) to monitor mood, anxiety and other behaviours from low (0) to high (5) levels.

2.5 Considerations in prescribing psychotropic medications for adults with DD:

- Adults with DD may be unable to communicate side effects of medications. They may also respond differently than those in the general population to psychotropic medication.

- They may have side effects at lower than usual doses.

- They may have idiosyncratic response to medication.

- They may have better responses to the newer SSRI antidepressants, associated with lower side effect profiles and anxiolytic properties.

- Adults with DD also have a higher rate of other physical conditions including sensory impairments (vision and hearing), cerebral palsy, epilepsy and other neurological disorders, cardiovascular and gastrointestinal problems, any of which, if present, will influence the choice of medication.

2.6 **Prescribing recommendations:**

- Where appropriate, start medications at lower than recommended doses and increase slowly, since some adults with DD may respond to lower than usual doses.

- Monitor for side effects by asking caregivers to indicate how clients might communicate or demonstrate a particular side effect (e.g., nausea) of a particular medication, given their frequently unique ways of manifesting bodily discomforts.

- Change one medication at a time and wait long enough for an effect.

- If starting another trial, withdraw previous trial medication slowly.

- If no response despite an adequate trial:
  – Review data collection and monitoring by caregivers
  – Review clinical hypothesis

- Look for new, and review existing, medical problems.

- Ensure that supports are appropriate and optimal to disability needs.

- Review psychiatric diagnoses.

2.7 **Documentation and review:**

- Maintain a record of all prescriptions, dates, changes, effectiveness and side effects.

- Review the psychiatric diagnostic or specific behavioural pharmacological justification for the long term use of psychotropic medications at least annually.

3. **Using PRN ("as needed") medication to manage acute episodes of behaviour disturbance for adults with DD** (Deb 2006)

3.1 As part of an overall treatment care plan that involves the patient, caregivers and appropriate persons providing consent, PRN medication may be prescribed.

3.2 In any such treatment plan, service agency protocols regarding PRN medications will need to be incorporated.

3.3 Record the reason for prescribing PRN medication in the notes. Set objectives for measuring outcomes over a specified period of time.

3.4 Monitor the PRN medication at regular intervals, with the time period for monitoring to be set when prescribing.

3.5 Note the indication for administering a PRN medication, the minimum interval between doses, and the maximum dose allowed in a 24-hour period.

3.6 Consider discontinuing any PRN medication that has not been used for six months or longer, unless there is a specific clinical reason to continue it, which should be noted e.g., rescue medications for status epilepticus or prolonged seizures or prolonged cluster of seizures.

3.7 Do not prescribe at any one time PRN psychotropic medications from more than one therapeutic category without stipulating the reasons.

3.8 Do not prescribe more than two medications for any one indication.

3.9 If prescribing more than one medication as PRN treatment, stipulate the order in which they should be administered.

3.10 If a PRN medication is being given regularly (e.g., daily), review and consider whether a regular prescription is required

3.11 Carefully monitor medications from the same therapeutic category that are used concurrently as regular and as PRN prescription in order to avoid the risk of (inadvertently) overdosing. (Ensure that the total daily dose of the regular and the PRN prescriptions do not exceed the maximum recommended daily dose.)

4. See also – Tools for the Primary Care of People with Developmental Disabilities (DD):

- *Auditing Psychotropic Medication Therapy*

- *Rapid Tranquillization of Adults with Crisis Behaviours*

- *A Guide to Understanding Behavioural Problems and Emotional Concerns*

- *Initial Management of Behavioural Crises in Family Medicine*

- *ABC (Antecedent-Behaviour-Consequence) Chart*

References
1. ABC (Antecedent-Behaviour-Consequence) Chart. Available at **www.peatni.org/directory/index.asp**. Accessed 15 Feb. 2010.

2. Banks R, Bush A, Baker P, Bradshaw J, Carpenter P, Deb S, et al. Challenging behaviour: a unified approach. CR 144. 2007; Available at **www.rcpsych.ac.uk/files/pdfversion/cr144.pdf**. Accessed 19 Aug. 2008.

3. Bradley E. Section IV: Depression in special populations. In: Guidelines for the diagnosis and pharmacological treatment of depression. 1st ed. Toronto: MUMS Publications Clearinghouse. 1999;39.

4. Deb S, Carulla LS, Barnhill J, Torr J, Bradley E, Bertelli M, et al. Problem behaviour in adults with intellectual disabilities: International guide for using medications, World Psychiatry 2009 Oct.;8:181-186.

5. Deb S, Clarke D, Unwin G. Using medication to manage behaviour problems among adults with a learning disability: Quick reference guide (QRG). 2006;29. Available at **www.ld-medication.bham.ac.uk/1qrg.pdf**. Accessed 15 Feb. 2010.

6. Sullivan WF, Berg JM, Bradley E, Cheetham T, Denton R, Heng J, Hennen B, Joyce D, Kelly M, Korossy M, Lunsky Y, McMillan S. Primary care of adults with developmental disabilities: Canadian consensus guidelines. Can Fam Physician 2011;57:541-53.

AUDITING PSYCHOTROPIC MEDICATION THERAPY

Name:

DOB:

	Yes	No	Not Sure
1. Has the patient been given a psychiatric diagnosis?	☐	☐	☐
2. Is an interdisciplinary assessment indicated for the concerns for which the medication is being used, and has it been carried out?	☐	☐	☐
3. Is medication treatment consistent with the diagnosis?	☐	☐	☐
4. If patient does not have a psychiatric diagnosis and is being treated for "behaviour problems" are guidelines for problem behaviours being followed?	☐	☐	☐
5. Is the patient capable of consenting to medication treatment? If capable, has he/she given consent? If not capable, has consent been obtained from his/ substitute decision maker?	☐	☐	☐
6. Has the patient and/or his/her substitute decision maker (SDM) been informed regarding anticipated therapeutic medication treatment effects and potential side effects?	☐	☐	☐
7. Has a proper medical assessment been carried out prior to iniitiating medication therapy?	☐	☐	☐
8. Have target behaviours against which to monitor medication effectiveness been defined?	☐	☐	☐
9. Is there a plan to measure these target behaviours objectively and systematically?	☐	☐	☐
10. Is the patient being regularly monitored for side effects?	☐	☐	☐
11. Is the patient receiving too many psychotropic agents?	☐	☐	☐
12. Is the patient being under-medicated?	☐	☐	☐
13. Is the patient being over-medicated?	☐	☐	☐
14. Is medication therapy being changed too rapidly?	☐	☐	☐
15. Are PRN and stat doses of medications being used excessively?	☐	☐	☐
16. Are patients treated with antipsychotic agents being regularly evaluated for tardive dyskinesia and metabolic syndrome?	☐	☐	☐
17. Have the psychotropic medication therapy and psychiatric diagnosis or special behavioural pharmacological justification for the medication been reviewed in the past year?	☐	☐	☐
18. Has a date been set for the next review?	☐	☐	☐

Comments/Action Plan (for issues flagged):

Date (dd/mm/yyyy): _____ **Signature:** _____

This tool was developed in recognition of the complexities of psychotropic medication use in adults with developmental disabilities (DD). Research has demonstrated that such medications are often overprescribed or otherwise inappropriately prescribed. This tool is intended to help primary care providers to audit psychotropic medication use in their patients with DD, so that such medications are used following best practice guidelines in this population.

Underlying the use of this tool is the concept of partnership with patients and caregivers in use of psychotropic medications, monitoring effectiveness, and any side effects of these medications.

As recommended in the *Primary Care of Adults with Developmental Disabilities: Canadian Consensus Guidelines* [1]:

- Medications should be reviewed **every three months, including indications, dosages, efficacy and side effects** [Guideline 5].
- Regularly audit the use of prescribed psychotropic medication, including those used PRN [Guideline 22].
- Review the psychiatric diagnosis and the appropriateness of prescribed medications for this diagnosis whenever there is a behaviour change [Guideline 27].
- Adults with DD may be unable to communicate side-effects and may also respond to psychotropic medications differently from those in the general population [Guideline 27].
- Reassess the need for ongoing use of antipsychotic medications at regular intervals and consider dose reduction or discontinuation when appropriate [Guideline 28].

Adapted from Sovner 1985 and Deb 2006 by the Behavioural and Mental Health Working Group, chaired by Dr. E. Bradley, Surrey Place Centre.

1. Sullivan WF, Berg JM, Bradley E, Cheetham T, Denton R, Heng J, Hennen B, Joyce D, Kelly M, Korossy M, Lunsky Y, McMillan S. Primary care of adults with developmental disabilities: Canadian consensus guidelines. Can Fam Physician 2011;57:541-53.

2. Sovner R, Hurley AD. Assessing the quality of psychotropic drug regimens prescribed for mentally retarded persons. Psych Aspects Ment Retard 1985 August/September; 4 (8/9):31-38.

3. Deb S, Clarke D, Unwin G. Using medication to manage behaviour problems among adults with a learning disability. 2006;36. **www.ld-medication.bham.ac.uk/1qrg.pdf**

Rapid Tranquillization of Adults with Crisis Behaviours

This tool was developed to help primary care providers in community and Emergency Department settings whose patients with DD are exhibiting crisis behaviours and require rapid tranquillization.

TABLE 1: GOALS AND CONSIDERATIONS IN RAPID TRANQUILLIZATION OF ADULTS WITH DD	
Goals	• Similar for all people exhibiting crisis behaviours, including those with DD. • Reduce agitation and associated risk of harm to the patient, and where applicable, to others, in the safest and least intrusive manner possible.
Specific Considerations regarding Psychotropic Medications for Adults with DD	• Should guide management decisions, including in crisis situations. • Often on multiple medications and at increased risk of adverse medication interactions. • Some may have atypical responses or side-effects at lower doses, and some cannot describe harmful or distressing effects of the medications that they are taking [1]. • Adults with DD associated with Autism Spectrum Disorders (ASD), about 30% of adults with DD, may react paradoxically to new psychotropic medications (e.g., when given a benzodiazepine, they may become agitated rather than sedated). • When considering psychotropic medications for adults with DD it is important to elicit their history with such medications and the patient's or caregivers preferences.
Initial treatment	• **Use a single medication initially, preferably a benzodiazepine at a sufficient dose** (e.g., lorazepam 4 mg), and wait the indicated time prior to repeating the dose. Experienced Emergency Department psychiatrists who work with adults with DD report that most crisis behaviours can be managed with **10 mg or less of lorazepam**. This is preferable when effective, as it avoids the distressing side effects that often accompany antipsychotics. • Given that antipsychotic medications are often inappropriately prescribed for adults with DD [1], reducing the exposure of adults with DD exhibiting crisis behaviours to these medications would help to mitigate this problem.

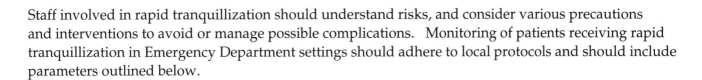

Staff involved in rapid tranquillization should understand risks, and consider various precautions and interventions to avoid or manage possible complications. Monitoring of patients receiving rapid tranquillization in Emergency Department settings should adhere to local protocols and should include parameters outlined below.

TABLE 2: RISKS, PRECAUTIONS, MONITORING	
Risks	• Over sedation • Respiratory depression • Cardiovascular complications (e.g., QT prolongation) • Acute dystonic reactions
Precautions	• Crash cart with bag-valve mask (BVM) and airway equipment available • Staff trained in Basic Life Support • Review prior EKG before introducing antipsychotic medications • Benztropine available for acute dystonic reactions • Flumazenil IV available for oversedation
Physical Monitoring	• Temperature (if increased, urgently assess for neuroleptic malignant syndrome) • Blood pressure • Pulse • Respiratory rate (with continuous pulse oxymetry in unresponsive patients)

TABLE 3A: INITIAL STEPS TO RAPID TRANQUILLIZATION [2]

	Modifying Circumstances	Choice(s)	Usual Oral Dosage	Notes
STEP 1	Attempt non-medication interventions, if appropriate	1. De-escalation 2. Time out in a safe seclusion room		
STEP 2	PATIENT IS ALREADY RECEIVING AN ORAL OR DEPOT ANTISYCHOTIC; AVOID GIVING ANOTHER ANTIPSYCHOTIC MEDICATION [a]	Lorazepam [d]	1-4 mg SL (sublingual)	Repeat once after 45-60 minutes if insufficient effect. Go to step 3 if two doses fail to produce desired effect or sooner if the patient or others are at significant risk for harm
	PATIENT IS NOT ALREADY RECEIVING AN ORAL OR DEPOT ANTISYCHOTIC OR IF PATIENT IS ACUTELY PSYCHOTIC [a,b,c]	Olanzapine [3] OR	10 mg PO	Rapidly dissolving form is Zydis ® **AVOID combining with lorazepam or other benzodiazepine [e]**
	AVOID combining two antipsychotics WAIT 4 hours before repeating same antipsychotic GO TO STEP 3 if second dose of lorazapam or antipsychotic fails to produce desired effect or sooner if the patient or others are at significant risk for harm	Quetiapine OR Risperidone [4, 5, 6, 7] OR Loxapine OR Haloperidol [b]	100-200 mg PO 1-2 mg PO 25 mg PO 5 mg PO	**ANY ONE of these CHOICES WITH or WITHOUT** **Lorazepam [d]** 1-4 mg SL (sublingual) Repeat lorazepam once after 45-60 minutes if insufficient effect

a. The choice of a new medication depends on other medications being taken. If the adult with DD is established on antipsychotic medications, lorazepam alone may be added. If the adult with DD is receiving benzodiazepines regularly, an antipsychotic alone may be added. Most patients respond best to a combination of an antipsychotic and lorazepam but an antipsychotic or benzodiazepine can also be used alone. Monitor vital signs as appropriate (see Table 2).

b. Before giving antipsychotics (particularly haloperidol) consider reviewing a prior EKG (or obtaining one), if possible, to assess the presence of QT prolongation. On an EKG, the QT interval should be less than 450-500 milliseconds.

c. **Due to the risk of acute dystonic reactions** (incidence is about 6% with haloperidol) ensure benztropine 1-2 mg IM or procyclidine 5-10 mg IM is available.

d. In patients receiving clozapine, lorazepam is contraindicated.

e. Combining olanzepine with lorazepam or other benzodiazepines should be avoided due to the risks of excessive sedation.

TABLE 3B: NEXT STEPS TO RAPID TRANQUILLIZATION – ADDITIONAL STEPS IN EMERGENCY DEPARTMENT AND HOSPITAL SETTINGS [f,g,h,i]

	Modifying Circumstances	Choice(s)	Usual IM Dosage	Notes
STEP 3	Oral therapy is refused, has failed or is insufficient for the level of crisis [f]	**Lorazepam** [8] OR	1-4mg IM Mix 1:1 with sterile saline	Flumazenil IV **should be available** for benzodiazepine-induced respiratory depression Flumenazil dosing [12] Initial: 0.2 mg IV over 15 seconds Max: 1 mg
		Olanzapine [i, 9, 10]	10 mg IM	**DO NOT combine** with IM benzodiazepine [11]
	If PO or IM antipsychotic given then WAIT 4 hours before repeating the same antipsychotic IM [f, g, h]	OR **Loxapine** OR **Haloperidol** [9, 10]	25 mg IM 5 mg IM	*Either **ONE** of these CHOICES WITH or WITHOUT* *Lorazepam* 1-2 mg IM Mix 1:1 with sterile saline **Use separate syringes for loxapine and lorazepam** **Repeat lorazepam 1-2 mg IM after 45-60 minutes if insufficient effect**
STEP 4	**Refractory severe symptoms** [j]	Consider intravenous (IV) medications (e.g., diazepam), the use of which is beyond the scope of these guidelines		

f. Consider intramuscular (IM) medication when oral therapy is refused, has failed or is insufficient for the level of crisis. Most patients respond best to a combination of an antipsychotic and lorazepam but an antipsychotic or benzodiazepine can also be used alone. Monitor vital signs as appropriate (see Table 2).

g. Before giving antipsychotics (particularly haloperidol) consider reviewing a prior EKG (or obtaining one), if possible, due to the risk of cardiac arrhythmias associated with QT prolongation. On an EKG, the QT interval should be less than 450-500 milliseconds. IM haloperidol should be considered a third line treatment option due to its increased risk of adverse effects.

h. **Due to the risk of acute dystonic reactions** (incidence is about 6% with haloperidol) ensure benztropine 1-2 mg IM or procyclidine 5-10 mg IM is available.

i. Recommended by National Institute for Clinical Excellence (NICE – UK) for moderately severe behavioural disturbance only.

j. **Refractory, severe symptoms:** a) Confirm the patient's incapacity to consent and document. Even if incapable, seek the patient's views on treatment options and their assent to a plan; b) Proceed with management while making efforts to involve his or her Substitute Decision Maker; c) Consult with an experienced colleague in psychopharmacology or anaesthesia.

Tool Development Process:

Primary care of adults with developmental disabilities: Canadian consensus guidelines [1] address considerations and make recommendations regarding the use of psychotropic medications for adults with developmental disabilities.

For development of this tool, guidelines on rapid tranquillization were reviewed. Currently there are no published standard Canadian guidelines regarding rapid tranquillization for the general population or for adults with DD. The recent paper of Taylor [2] from the United Kingdom, which gave recommendations for management of acutely disturbed behaviour involving mainly the non-DD population, was used as a base. Emergency physicians and psychiatrists with clinical expertise in DD-specific considerations in rapid tranquillization were consulted and their input was incorporated. Recommendations were adapted to reflect common practices and available medications in Canada.

Adapted from Taylor [2] by William F. Sullivan MD and David Joyce MD.

Thanks to the following physicians and pharmacist for their review and helpful input:
Ian Dawe MD, Jody Lofchy MD, Frank Martino MD, Elspeth Bradley MD and Laurie Dunn MSc, BScPhm.

References

1. Sullivan WF, Berg JM, Bradley E, Cheetham T, Denton R, Heng J, Hennen B, Joyce D, Kelly M, Korossy M, Lunsky Y, McMillan S. Primary care of adults with developmental disabilities: Canadian consensus guidelines. Can Fam Physician 2011;57:541-53.

2. Taylor D, Paton C, Kerwin R. Acutely disturbed or violent behaviour. In: Taylor D, Paton C, Kerwin R, editors. The Maudsley prescribing guidelines. 10th ed. London: Informa Healthcare; 2009. p. 417-422.

3. Simpson JR, Jr, Thompson CR, Beckson M. Impact of orally disintegrating olanzapine on use of intramuscular antipsychotics, seclusion, and restraint in an acute inpatient psychiatric setting. J Clin Psychopharmacol 2006 Jun;26(3):333-335.

4. Currier GW, Chou JC, Feifel D, Bossie CA, Turkoz I, Mahmoud RA, et al. Acute treatment of psychotic agitation: a randomized comparison of oral treatment with risperidone and lorazepam versus intramuscular treatment with haloperidol and lorazepam. J Clin Psychiatry 2004 Mar;65(3):386-394.

5. Currier GW, Simpson GM. Risperidone liquid concentrate and oral lorazepam versus intramuscular haloperidol and intramuscular lorazepam for treatment of psychotic agitation. J Clin Psychiatry 2001 Mar;62(3):153-157.

6. Lejeune J, Larmo I, Chrzanowski W, Witte R, Karavatos A, Schreiner A, et al. Oral risperidone plus oral lorazepam versus standard care with intramuscular conventional neuroleptics in the initial phase of treating individuals with acute psychosis. Int Clin Psychopharmacol 2004 Sep;19(5):259-269.

7. Yildiz A, Turgay A, Alpay M, Sachs GS. Observational data on the antiagitation effect of risperidone tablets in emergency settings: A preliminary report. Int J Psychiatry Clin Pract 2003 Sep;7(3):217-221.

8. Alexander J, Tharyan P, Adams C, John T, Mol C, Philip J. Rapid tranquillisation of violent or agitated patients in a psychiatric emergency setting. Pragmatic randomised trial of intramuscular lorazepam v. haloperidol plus promethazine. Br J Psychiatry 2004 Jul;185:63-69.

9. Breier A, Meehan K, Birkett M, David S, Ferchland I, Sutton V, et al. A double-blind, placebo-controlled dose-response comparison of intramuscular olanzapine and haloperidol in the treatment of acute agitation in schizophrenia. Arch Gen Psychiatry 2002 May;59(5):441-448.

10. National Institute for Health and Clinical Excellence (NICE). Violence – the short-term management of disturbed/violent behaviour in in-patient psychiatric settings and emergency departments. Clinical Guideline 25. Royal College of Nursing February 2005. Available from **www.nice.org.uk/CG025**.

11. Zacher JL, Roche-Desilets J. Hypotension secondary to the combination of intramuscular olanzapine and intramuscular lorazepam. J Clin Psychiatry 2005 Dec;66(12):1614-1615.

12. Canadian Drug Reference for Health Professionals (CPS). CPHA. Ottawa. 2011. pg. 184.

COMMENT SHEET

We welcome your participation in the revision to the tools by receiving your comments and recommendations on how to improve them. You may also submit an on-line form which is available at: **www.mumshealth.com/content/order_forms/guideline_comment_sheet.pdf**.

ITEM		COMMENTS
1. Are these tools easy to understand and helpful?	☐ Yes ☐ No	
2. Would you recommend any content changes or new topics for tools?	☐ Yes ☐ No	
3. Would you recommend any format changes?	☐ Yes ☐ No	
4. Do you find this book useful for helping to manage your patients with DD?	☐ Yes ☐ No	
5. Any other comments, suggestions or additional topics?		

Please provide a return address, fax, telephone number and e-mail if you would like:

☐ updates
☐ to participate in a future MUMS Guidelines Panel
☐ interested in seeing an app (iphone) for Anti-Infective Guideline

THANK YOU

Name: _____

Address: _____

_____

Telephone: _____

Fax: _____

Email: _____

Please return to:
MUMS GUIDELINE CLEARINGHOUSE
www.mumshealth.com
Suite 200 - 301 Donlands Ave., Toronto M4J 3R8
fax (416) 597-8574 (toll-free 1-866-540-1847) or e-mail: guidelines@mumshealth

NOTES